Unleashed

"In a distinctively and beautifully feminine manner, Sonja Corbitt addresses one of the fundamental questions we all ask, 'What is the purpose of my life?' And she helps the reader discover the answer with scripture, experiences from her own journey, and a foundational reliance upon the love of the Holy Spirit. You will not be the same person after reading this book."

Scott Russell
Director
Saint Joseph Communications

"It's hard to find a topic in the Christian life more inclined to bewilderment and fear than who the Holy Spirit is and how he moves. With gentleness and humility, Sonja Corbitt has sent away this misunderstood ghost and revealed the Counselor. The gift of this book is that it will lead each serious reader to a greater gift—self-knowledge—and from there, on to a still greater gift—an understanding of how the Holy Spirit works in our lives and how we can best cooperate with him; see his handiwork; and reap all the joy, healing, and blessing he longs to give. Sonja offers simple yet powerful steps even those just beginning their faith journey can take to unleash the power of God . . . and be amazed at what he does."

Jennifer Hartline
Columnist
Catholic Online

"*Unleashed* is a breathtaking journey through the scriptures where author Sonja Corbitt connects the power of the Bible to everyday life experiences. With a wonderful freshness and ease that is both engaging and enlightening, *Unleashed* will stir your heart and lift your soul. This book will equip you with the spiritual tools necessary to build the dynamic, joy-filled relationship with Jesus Christ that you've always wanted. Very highly recommended!"

Deacon Harold Burke-Sivers
EWTN host
Author of *The Mass in Sacred Scripture*

How to Receive
Everything the
Holy Spirit
Wants to
Give You

A Catholic Woman's Walk with Scripture

Sonja Corbitt

AVE MARIA PRESS AVE Notre Dame, Indiana

Nihil Obstat: Rev. Jayd D. Neely, *Censor Librorum*

Imprimatur: Most Rev. David R. Choby, Bishop of Nashville

               December 15, 2014

Founded in 1865, Ave Maria Press is a ministry of the United States Province of Holy Cross.

www.avemariapress.com

Paperback: ISBN-13 978-1-59471-599-0

E-book: ISBN-13 978-1-59471-600-3

Cover image © Stocksy.com.

Cover and text design by Katherine Robinson.

Printed and bound in the United States of America.

Library of Congress Cataloging-in-Publication Data is available.

To Ginna, who lent me her faith,

Bob, who lent me his freedom,

Lee, who lent me his hospitality,

and Mary, who lent me her "yes."

Contents

Foreword

It was the start of a new school year, in a new city, with new people. We had moved our family from the security of a hometown that felt comfortable and familiar, and we were starting all over. Insecurity, fear of the unknown, and apprehension nipped at our heels as we prepared to make this new place home. The night before school began, we took our kids down to the beach and watched them play. Encountering the waves, the beauty of creation, and the irresistible pull of the water unleashed them to just enjoy the moment. Joy. Peace. Laughter. Everyone soaked up the happiness and freedom and momentarily forgot their worries. If only we could have bottled up what was felt that evening and sprinkled it over everyone as they headed out the door to face their daily challenges. But the daily grind greets us, and without realizing it we start living for the next blissful break instead of appreciating the sacredness of every moment.

How many of us are living for the next vacation? Or just waiting for the next season of life? Or have convinced ourselves that we can't experience freedom and joy until some circumstance changes? I believe most of us feel stuck in these places. In my years of leading Walking with Purpose, I have spoken with woman after woman who longs for something bound up in her heart to be unleashed and freed. Sometimes it's a hidden passion and purpose. Other times it's a habitual sin that she can't break free from. Or it's just a general restlessness—a sense that there is more—but that something more seems illusive.

What if the key to experiencing freedom and joy wasn't found in idyllic circumstances but, instead, in a steady connection to the Holy Spirit? What if there was something that God wants to unleash in our lives that could transform us from within? In *Unleashed*, Sonja Corbitt helps women receive everything the Holy Spirit is longing to pour over us. Her love of scripture and ability to present it in a way that is immensely practical helps us to look at the places in our lives that are bound up and in need of release. She comes alongside us as a friend and as a woman who is still on the journey. Her wisdom comes from experience, but it is never presented in a spirit of "just get your act together and learn from me." She has been there. She is real. In these pages, we find a kindred spirit who offers a hand to help us up. She understands how hard life can be. Yet she goes beyond saying, "I know what the struggle feels like." By God's grace, Sonja has experienced victory and moved past some of the pitfalls a lot of us are still in. Her words give us tools to move forward and experience the life we were created for.

When we struggle with discontentment over our circumstances, we are all tempted to numb that discomfort in all sorts of ways. Sonja challenges us, instead, to do the deep soul work that will ultimately lead to freedom and satisfaction.

She begins by inviting us to unleash the Holy Spirit to reframe our stories. Not a single heartache in our lives has been wasted. God has seen every tear and wants to use everything we have experienced in order to achieve his purposes in our lives and world. There's no need to wallow in regret. Once we are forgiven, we are free for God to redeem every mistake. A part of the process of unleashing will require forgiveness of others. Our stories haven't occurred in isolation. People have hurt us, and many of us are bound by resentment and bitterness. Sonja challenges us to surrender judgment and receive peace in exchange.

We can all point to experiences in our lives when we have been confused by what God was doing and allowing. Perhaps we've wondered if he was asleep on the job. In dark moments, we may question whether or not he even cares. This is sacred ground. This is where our deepest hurts reside, and the question why makes healing and moving forward seem impossible. Sonja guides us to look at our circumstances and helps us probe them for lessons that lead us toward the process of purification, to hear God more clearly, and to grow in maturity.

Another place so many of us are stuck is in the area of passion and purpose. We might wonder why we are here. We wonder if we really matter. We feel desires within and wonder if following God means squelching them. If we're supposed to be other-focused, should we just set our own hopes aside? Never has there been a time when women have had more advantages, yet our level of discontentment is sky-high. We wonder what we are missing. These are good things to wrestle with, because make no mistake: we were made for more. God has big plans for each one of us, and our desires are a big part of that.

God wants us to ask the scary questions. He wants to travel with us to our places of discontentment and the places where we dream. Calling us away from the sleep of complacency, God asks us to take his hand and step out into the deep. The alternative is to scurry back to a place of familiarity. In Sonja's words, "ultimately, comfort seeking is a denial of the need to change." When we refuse to change, we miss out on becoming the women God created us to be. We miss out, and the world misses out. God created each of his precious daughters and gave us a mission when we were still in the womb. Those things that cause us to jump off the couch in righteous indignation? Those needs that we see around us? God is waiting for us to wake up and recognize that the things that wreck our hearts wreck his as well. He asks us to take the time to come to a place of spiritual wholeness so we can get on to the business of being his hands and feet to our desperate, aching world.

The truths contained in *Unleashed,* if taken to heart and applied, can release our souls to receive God in his fullness. New patterns of behavior and thought can be created. Freedom will no longer be a fanciful dream, but a daily experience. You do not have to finish the way that you started.

So read this precious book with an open heart. Ask the Holy Spirit to prepare you to receive his truth. Ask him to cover your hurts with a protective balm so that you can work through the layers of your heart, bit by bit. Be assured, the lover of your soul is gentle. He is for you. He is Goodness Itself. Don't be afraid of the journey. He is there with you, each step of the way.

Lisa Brenninkmeyer
Founder of Walking with Purpose
Author of *Walking with Purpose: Seven Priorities That Make Life Work*

Introduction

Most of the time, doesn't discussion or exploration of the Holy Spirit involve lots of intimidation with reticence on top, if it occurs at all? Is it because we are afraid to be "haunted" by the *Holy Ghost*? Or perhaps it's because we know our dried-up lives are nothing if they aren't perfect kindling for a burning bush and we probably shouldn't get too close.

I remember pouting to God once about having to be my husband's "helper." You know, in Genesis 2:18 where God says, "It is not good that the man should be alone; I will make him a helper fit for him," and then he makes Eve for Adam? I thought, *Why does he get to do all the* doing *that gets done, and I just get to "help"?* Silly and immature, I know.

But God said to me, "I am The Helper." And he is.

In St. John's gospel Jesus says, "I will pray the Father, and he will give you another Counselor, to be with you for ever, even the Spirit of truth" (Jn 14:16–17). Other versions translate *Counselor* as Advocate, Helper, Paraclete, or Comforter. It's a battle word that conveys the idea of coming alongside, to surround, advise, guard, protect, and aid.

Because it is part of our feminine genius, women do this for others as a reflection of the Holy Spirit who humbly does it for us all. In fact it's only *because* of him that I can *help* anyone. I imitate him, the Great Helper, and as I do I am drawn into a deep, fertile relationship with the Holy Spirit that has the stamp of his character. This idea is very Marian, for Mary has an utterly unique, fertile, and practical relationship with the Holy Spirit.

Every time I present the "Unleashed" talk at conferences and retreats, I am almost mobbed afterward by people on a similar journey, with comparable agonies, terrible habits, toxic relationships, and repetitive circumstances that bind and burden us all. I wrote this book to offer how the Holy Spirit came alongside and unleashed me through the scriptures, to help you get in touch with him through the surprisingly practical ways he comes alongside and teaches me. This book may be more meditation than scripture study, per se. I probably take a different approach than some authors you've read or scripture studies you've done. There's room for us all at the table of the Word, right? Because it's full of scripture *and* study, it's a feast for groups and individuals. But I hope you find studying the scriptures with me less intimidating than spinach and maybe even as tasty as a cupcake.

Ever practical and real like Mary, we're going to hear God speak, ponder his word in our hearts, and act decisively on what he says. The foundation of each chapter is a question that Jesus asked in the scriptures, questions Jesus asks each of us personally. Expect each chapter (except the first) to also include:

- A Review—"Repetition is the mother of learning," as they say, so we spend some time revisiting each chapter in a concise way.
- An Invitation—This section applies the scriptures and the chapter to our own lives.
- A God Prompt—Here I offer specific ways to get personally and directly in touch with God.

I invite you now to consider marking your book as you read and to make notes in a journal of some sort as you go. You might be surprised at what bubbles up to the surface as you read and meditate. I also suggest reading *Unleashed* with a Bible on hand, perhaps the *Catechism*, too, especially if you're reading and studying as a group. That will be helpful, but it's not necessary. The Invitation and God Prompt sections might be too personal for group sharing, so there are group study questions and a supplemental leader's guide located in the back of the book just for you and your group.

That's about it. So, come sit here beside me, and let's chat. And have a cupcake.

1

*W*hat Do You Wish?

Matthew 20:21, NAB

Come On In, Lord.
Unleash Your Spirit!

The day it clicked was like a tiny mental gear I hadn't known existed sliding gently into place. Both a new Catholic and new homeschooling parent, I was still in my pajamas, eating raspberries and cheddar for breakfast while facilitating a history lesson for my third-grade son. He was working on a timeline review that included the Creation event; dinosaurs and evolution; the Sumerian civilization and its cuneiform writing; Egyptian civilization, pharaohs, and the pyramids; and Moses's Exodus.

Suddenly, seeing all of these events side by side on the same timeline made me realize that secular and biblical history are the same history, and my own human past. No

1

longer two separate collections of stories that happened thousands of years ago, all those Bible "stories" I had grown up with in church and the "stories" of early civilizations from public school suddenly became one history, and *real* in a way they hadn't seemed before. The people came alive when I imagined them all living together on our common arc of time, which included me and my own family.

Even though scriptural genres can be highly literary and poetic, our sacred history is true. What if I began to read scripture with the thought that they are my people, that they are me? What if I read it remembering I will be those people for future generations, whether for good or ill?

In this chapter we consider a question Jesus asked the mother of two of his disciples: "What do you wish?" (Mt 20:21). An eyewitness account of a real person's conversation with Jesus, here St. Matthew conveys the mother's considerable ambition for her sons. She asked Jesus for places of power and authority in the kingdom of God for them.

If the Holy Spirit gave *you* such a wish, what would it be? Twenty pounds gone overnight? A miraculous conversion or healing of a loved one? Relief from an addiction? Greater financial security? A restored relationship?

For most of us, our wishes could probably be distilled to a single seven-letter word: freedom—freedom from sickness, death, worry. We want to be freed from the regrets, habits, and painful encounters in our lives that rob us of peace and joy. Like the mother in this gospel, isn't my single greatest wish for myself and my children simply to be fulfilled? Don't I also go to great lengths to make it possible for them?

In this chapter and those following, we'll listen in on some conversations that Jesus had with real people like you and me. Among the many things Jesus did, he asked a lot of probing questions. Because the scriptures are real and true for us in our time, too, we'll place ourselves in the narrative. As we hear him ask us those same questions, we're going to answer them, because a question from Jesus is always an invitation to *unleash* and to *be unleashed*.

Along the way, I hope we'll also discover the secret to true fulfillment: turning the Holy Spirit loose in our hearts and giving him permission to identify and eradicate the causes of our worry, unhappiness, discontent, and regret. It all begins with a simple act of hospitality. By answering Jesus' questions, we invite God in to throw open the doors and windows of our hearts and lives, and to unleash his Word to shine a strong, clear light that dispels the darkness.

Creating a Happy Home for God

Few things say "home" to me like the smell of early spring floating through a screen door and open windows—windows that look out over acres of clover and ambling flocks. Such a breeze makes lacey curtains blow greenness into rooms and the scent of daffodils into sheets billowing on the line—sheets that will soon cradle exhausted bodies flopping in feather beds with fluffy comforters. Can you see yourself in a home like this?

Hospitality is often understood as a way of entertaining. In fact, hospitality is a whole industry—think Martha Stewart, Ina Garten, Giada De Laurentiis, and Williams-Sonoma. Because I completely lack the hospitality gene, the exhortation, "Do not neglect hospitality, for through it some have unknowingly entertained angels" (Heb 13:2, NAB) used to fill me with trepidation. It always brought to mind welcoming that one special guest at Thanksgiving or Christmas—you know, the one you couldn't wait to bid good-bye? Don't we all have those kinds of people in our lives? Bless their hearts.

No, southern hospitality doesn't always come naturally to me. I'm a Secular Carmelite in formation; I have a hermetical streak a canyon wide. There was a time when I could barely tolerate the thought of entertaining certain relatives, much less strangers. I adore people with gifts of hospitality for their warmth, generosity, sensitivity, and openness. But to me, hospitality was simply a lot of work tending toward a brewing conflict.

And yet, whether you have a hermetical inclination or a love for entertaining, hospitality has spiritual as well as social associations. In Jewish thought, hospitality was modeled by God, who created the cosmos and world to welcome the human race, the "other." Think about the Holy Family, in which hospitality was a simple, constantly repeated "yes" that welcomed each "other."

As Christians we are invited to consider hospitality as using what's been given to welcome Christ. Through the Nativity and Holy Family we learn that hospitality means to prepare a space for Christ—in the home, sure, but primarily in the heart. We will see this repeatedly in the following chapters: Jesus is always ready to receive the other and wants to be received. He asks the question and anticipates the answer. I confess I find this understanding of hospitality much easier and far less stressful to apply.

It's fun to have tea parties, beautiful linens, bone china, modern furniture, and a perfect home when you welcome others. But I began to find that those things sometimes became an obstacle to accepting and reaching others in need. We can't invite so-and-so because they aren't the right people, or we don't have the right dishes or the perfect house, the amount of time, the personality, and so on.

The Benedictine charism is especially good at expressing the scriptural understanding of hospitality, in which all things are not mine, only on loan—even spiritual "things." St. Benedict tells us to enjoy our things, but release and return them. We don't possess them.

He speaks about the interior disposition of the heart. He emphasizes attitude, an attitude of detachment—or better, nonattachment. Benedict is clear that outward hospitality and conformity don't count. There must be integrity between the exterior and the interior—and this unity is primary. I have to let my things go free. They don't own me; I am not in bondage to them. And I do not own them. I handle them with care, respect, and with all courtesy of love and offer them back to Christ from whom I first received them.

Biblical hospitality is simply sharing all that has been given to me with those I have been given. As I do so, I welcome Christ and unleash his spirit: "As you did it to one of the least of these my brethren, you did it to me" (Mt 25:40). For the Holy Family, this primarily meant the domestic church, their home. For us, throughout our time together, I'd like you to think of your heart and life as the primary places to share what you have, no matter the condition, with Jesus. Such simplicity of heart is an invitation and incubator for Christ to grow in "wisdom and stature" in the little Nazareth home of the spirit (Lk 2:52).

As I began to learn the meaning of hospitality through the simplicity of the Holy Family, a particular man came clearly and repeatedly to mind. An older solitary man, he always sat in the pew with us at Mass, and he worked at our supermarket as a courtesy clerk. I saw him every Friday at the grocery store and beside me every Sunday in the church pew, but I had never really talked to him. I felt called to invite him to Sunday dinner. We learned he does not drive and walks to Mass each week, so we took him home with us, twenty-five miles out of town, for our Sunday-dinner-and-afternoon-porch routine. We discovered Lex lives with and cares for his mother, is a war veteran, had a passionate love relationship that never worked out and left him unmarried, takes a taxi to work every day, and is a wealth of genealogical information on our county and region. He is a fascinating man who was visibly delighted by being with our family, but I would never have known the surprise and pleasure of him as a person if I had not attempted to apply the hospitality lesson.

I give what I have and find myself enriched and even surprised. For me, that is a refreshing understanding of hospitality because it cares nothing for what the condition of the house, dishes, linens, or children are like at all. While Christ doesn't need our hospitality, he waits to be surprised because it is a gift. I love the idea I might be able to surprise God (however loosely I have to apply the principle to his omniscience).

Godly "Remodeling"

My husband and I have been living in and remodeling a romantic old farmhouse for almost the entire twenty years of our marriage. When we first moved in, I had great expectations for how quickly and smoothly the work would go. Every room needed to be gutted and rebuilt from the foundation up. In the beginning I struggled against how long the process would remain unfinished (forever!).

Now I clearly see God has used my house to teach me important, surprising lessons on the differences between needs and wants, simplicity, patience, and the wonder of beautiful things that are imperfect but still useful and interesting. I purposely kept a couple of our ancient interior walls with their gorgeous, peeling wallpaper simply for their disheveled beauty. I regularly repurpose antiques and other items that are too damaged for their original functions in ways that are surprising and even funny: I use an old iron headboard as a garden gate, a flowerpot to corral kitchen utensils, and a marble bust as a handy perch for hats and caps.

Once I began to see our house as a metaphor for my life with God, living and resting in his provision, then offering others hospitality in an unfinished house became much easier and more enjoyable. My heart was unleashed unto true hospitality.

When I apply scriptural hospitality, I discover that I must simply give God all I have—in heart, home, habits, relationships, circumstances, desires, and prayer—and open wide myself to the surprise and freedom that happens when the Holy Spirit is unleashed through it all.

At first, my own destructive patterns prevented a total welcoming and full-hearted yes to the Lord in a lot of areas. Because it all desperately lacked spiritual propriety, I was unable, unwilling, and afraid to give what I had to the Holy Spirit. I didn't know, then, that opening my spiritual home and all its unkempt, disheveled rooms to him is the only way they can be freshened and freed. Since then, giving whatever I have and unleashing him—that exquisite, terrifying Divine—to move and work in my life has been a constant surprise and thrill.

It's a lot like fishing, isn't it? Or really, more like being caught? That seizing moment, the sudden sense of "startlement," and then the fierce awareness as the mental line springs taut, and the heart and mind are caught in fascination by some new consideration. For me it began with a tender conversation with my aunt about her relationship with God. I distinctly remember my near revulsion when she said she always imagined crawling up into the Father's lap when she prayed.

Not that I didn't long to be in my own father's lap, but my relationship with him involved a terrified respect, assurance of punishment, and extreme wariness confused up in the longing. I was unable to grasp wallowing happily around in Almighty God's lap or being there at all unless he was compelling me to. I was fascinated, but suspicious, in bondage to my beliefs about what God was like. Would I smell his heavenly Chaps cologne? Would he tickle me till it hurt? Would I then cry and wish I hadn't risked it? Would I say something that angered him and made him push me out?

Talking to my aunt, I remembered the curious story of David, shepherd boy and second king of Israel, said to be a man after God's own heart (Acts 13:21–22). Something about that possibility also intrigued me since I was always attempting to please my own father. Could the Almighty Father be pleased to such a degree? What would it take?

King David mounted a campaign to bring the Ark of the Covenant to Jerusalem. At that point in my life, the two most important matters in my consideration of the episode were that the Ark was where the presence of God rested—it was his throne—and that David stripped down to a linen garment and publicly leaped and danced before the Lord (2 Sm 6:14–16). I could not imagine what in the world could make David so happy about the Holy Spirit resting on that Ark that he felt unleashed enough to whirl and spin joyfully before the Lord, or how that made him a man after God's own heart, but I wanted to know. If it was possible to be so comfortable with him that I could climb in his lap and be carried in his bosom, I wanted it. I was hooked by the possibilities. In the simplest act of hospitality, I told him I wished to be released from all my doubt and fear and anger, and I opened my pitiful heart to him.

Over time, I came to understand that God longs to unleash me from all that hinders him from bounding to me with fulfillment; he waits patiently for the invitation to unleash his Spirit into my life. He is always speaking and working, asking me, "What do you wish?"; I just don't always see or hear or trust him. Maybe I worry he will churn through my life like a tornado, or shake the foundations of my life like an earthquake. Ah, but there is power in hearing him, no matter how he speaks.

For Those with Ears to Hear

And he said, "Go forth, and stand upon the mount before the Lord." And behold, the Lord

> passed by, and a great and strong wind rent the
> mountains, and broke in pieces the rocks before
> the Lord, but the Lord was not in the wind; and
> after the wind an earthquake, but the Lord was
> not in the earthquake; and after the earthquake a
> fire, but the Lord was not in the fire; and after the
> fire a still small voice. And when Elijah heard it,
> he wrapped his face in his mantle and went out
> and stood at the entrance of the cave. And behold,
> there came a voice to him, and said, "What are
> you doing here, Elijah?" (1 Kgs 19:11–13)

What are *you* doing here, Dear One? "What do you
wish?" Whatever has drawn you to this moment, it is ultimately God's "still small voice" beckoning you, just as he
spoke to Elijah in the cave on the mountain before sending
him to continue his prophetic work.

When we don't hear God, could it be because we
are looking for whirlwinds and earthquakes and burning
bushes, when usually he is continually speaking through
a still small voice that we are drowning out with regular
noise, anxieties, busyness, disillusions, and preconceptions?
What if part of the still small voice whispers in our patterns:
patterns of behavior, relationship, circumstance, and desire?
What if he is speaking to us, daily, through the scriptures
too?

Our God is a God of order, reason, and organization.
Just look closely at the diversity, great logic, and order of cre-
ation, for instance. One of my favorite examples is fractals.
Fractals are mathematical sets that self-repeat. Notice in a
Koch snowflake how the simple triangle shape is continu-
ally repeated to make more and more complicated patterns.
Yet each large pattern can ultimately be reduced to a basic
triangle.

The simple pattern is multiplied to become more complicated, and the complicated pattern is simplified, macro

and micro. Tree branches repeat in patterns. Flower petals
repeat in patterns. DNA repeats in patterns. Your life and
behavior repeats in patterns. Behavior patterns can get bigger and more complicated (and usually more painful) or be
reduced to their simplest, clearest terms.

God is not the author of confusion but of order (1 Cor
14:33). What if today, even now, God is speaking and working in your life through the order of your patterns? What
if recognizing those patterns is an invitation to work with
God there? This was Jesus' own habit—discerning where
God was working and joining him there. "Truly, truly, I say
to you, the Son can do nothing of his own accord, but only
what he sees the Father doing; for whatever he does, that the
Son does likewise. For the Father loves the Son, and shows
him all that he himself is doing" (Jn 5:19–20).

Because I didn't yet know him and his ways, I felt God
purposely hid understanding from me, and still there may
be times when he does and must. But Jesus seemed to think
God wants to let us know what he is up to in our lives so
we can cooperate with him. Take a look at Genesis 18:17–19:

> The LORD said, "Shall I hide from Abraham what I
> am about to do, seeing that Abraham shall become
> a great and mighty nation, and all the nations of
> the earth shall bless themselves by him? No, for I
> have chosen him, that he may charge his children
> and his household after him to keep the way of
> the LORD by doing righteousness and justice; so
> that the LORD may bring to Abraham what he has
> promised him."

This passage suggests the Holy Spirit wants you to know
what he is doing in your heart and circumstances so he
can bring to you what "he has promised." What has he
promised?

Your Promised Land

Some negative patterns are obvious to us and require both our cooperation and discipline as well as God's grace to conquer. However, because the soul is an abyss of mystery, there is deeper work to be done. *Salvation* in the scriptures is synonymous with *shalom,* or peace. It's a great big, full, *unleashed* word, meaning integration, wholeness, fulfillment, and sanctification. Not merely about behavior, salvation and peace involve motivations, and often these are buried deep in denial and the subconscious.

The more strongly I followed God, the more intimate I became with him. This intimacy quickly grew uncomfortable, however, when God began to challenge my deepseated distortions about who he is and what he is like. The ever-expanding circle of self-knowledge I began to attain in my walk with God was sometimes supremely burdensome, especially as I discerned that most of my worst behaviors and emotional binges stemmed from the same root; the depth of the root frightened me for my helplessness to reach or even detect it at all times. I worried I would never uproot it completely. I got so *sick* of going around the same mountain, time after time, and sometimes felt it would never be over. People told me that's just the way life is. We should all simply go about the business of doing our best and look forward to heaven when God will make everything okay.

However, I found the problem with that mentality is that if we do what we always did, we'll get what we always got. The Church teaches that we grow throughout our journeys in ways that merit reward, as well. While God will purify and make well in heaven what is not okay now, if we neglect progressing now while we live, our souls will remain tight and constricted, allowing only a little of God in.

Life is meant to expand us, to heal us, to widen our capacity and make us capable of accepting, receiving, holding, and communicating more of God, who is our "exceedingly great" unleashed reward (Gn 15:1)! What a small reward we receive if we are stingy in progressing and go to heaven with a stunted, immature capacity for receiving and enjoying God.

The Church's understanding of life's purpose is ultimately to increase our capacity for receiving him. Pope Francis said, "God's will is that we grow in our capacity to welcome one another, to forgive and to love, and to resemble Jesus. This is the holiness of the Church."[1]

To stop progressing is to say no to more of God. That's not why you're holding this book!

The letter to the Hebrews in the New Testament warns of the peril of not progressing. At first Christianity was Jewish. Jesus and the disciples were Jewish. Their meetings took place in the synagogues, and the first Church controversies involved adherence to Jewish laws. The first persecutors of the Church were those who felt Jesus and the apostles had hijacked their religion and were distorting it in blasphemous ways. Quickly, choosing to follow Christ became a life or death proposition. Christians were given over to the government to be persecuted, tortured, and martyred, and the temptation to return to the familiar safety of Judaism proved too strong for some to bear.

The letter to the Hebrews was written to those in danger of turning back. The author gives a pep talk, and one of the first scriptural examples offered as encouragement is the Israelites' wilderness journey to the Promised Land (Heb 3).

Be Not Afraid

The original account in Numbers 13 and 14 describes how God's people journeyed with him, following him out of the slavery of Egypt through the desert, all the way to the boundary of the Promised Land. Upon reaching the boundary, they sent in spies to determine what they could about the people and cities and bring back some of the fruit of the land.

We know what it's like to walk far longer than we ever planned, in scorching summer heat, with a parched tongue, gnawing stomach, and no end in sight. When the children of Israel got to that Promised Land, it was all they had fantasized about for years. Reporting on the abundance and fruitfulness of the land that God had promised them, they brought back the largest cluster of grapes ever seen and finally understood what God had meant when he said it was a land "flowing with milk and honey" (Ex 3:8). The phrase is a scriptural slogan that later became synonymous with God's goodness and promise of redemption in the land of *Kadesh*, meaning "holy."

Undoubtedly the phrase inspired visions of pleasure and plenty for the Israelites who had endured years of deprivation and something of a "cutback" in their standard of living in Egypt. Surely they imagined something equal to bonbons and weekends at the lake without a care in the world.

After the arid wilderness, Canaan was an exponentially good land, yet in the face of the obvious fruitfulness and rest of their imminent reward for following God, the spies abruptly focused on the troubles of the land—the fortification of its cities, the strength of the inhabitants, and their gigantic size. Steadfast in their bad report, they described the land as evil and its inhabitants unconquerable, a scandalous description that attacked the Giver of the land himself.

The people wept at the loss of their dream, a dream initiated by God, sure in the firm belief they had made a grave mistake in leaving slavery behind. What followed, the writer of the Hebrews concludes, was the tragic forfeit of the Promised Land altogether. They succumbed to fear at the threshold of the promise. They aborted their dream.

These episodes in Hebrew history are referred to over and over in the scriptures as a warning to us against tempting God. Jesus uses this account to defend against temptation (Mt 4:7) and reasoned with the disciples continually about their fears, "Why are you afraid? Have you no faith?" (Mk 4:40).

Through these scriptures, the Holy Spirit is telling us, over and over, that the paralysis of fear is unfaith, or unbelief. The psalmist says it is people who go astray in their hearts who do not persevere to the end, and calls such a departure a leaving of God himself. Such deserters do not know God's ways (Ps 95:10), the psalmist says, in foreboding tones. How can this be, if fear is a normal, human emotion?

Most of us are led by our emotions, yet the Holy Spirit invites us to be led by him through our will, made in his image, and therefore free. We must make faith the engine and emotion the caboose. When the Holy Spirit does give a strong feeling of his presence, is there anything better in the entire world? But it will be important to keep in mind throughout this book what our Church's doctors and theologians have taught for millennia: except for the Incarnate Son, God is pure, uncreated Spirit. Invisible. There's nothing to see, hear, sense, or feel of God at all unless he somehow takes a form. If we "feel" him at all, it is because he makes himself felt. Our feelings, then, are insufficient and unreliable guides in discerning God's action and activity. We have to look for other telltale signs, especially in our patterns.

Then, fear must be willfully conquered by trust—trust in what God says, trust in his goodness and purpose. When we trust, we love. When we trust, we have a hold of God. For this reason, the writer of Hebrews goes so far as to say that succumbing to fear is evil (3:12–14), "For we share in Christ, if *only* we hold our first confidence firm to the end . . ." (emphasis added). The Israelites refused to enter the Promised Land, and the decision is said to have been made because of unbelief (Heb 3:18–19).

They did not trust; they did not persevere; they let go and left God. In fact, the biblical authors give this event two titles, *Meribah*, meaning rebellion, and *Massah*, meaning tempted (Heb 3:8). The notorious, fatal offense was fear. Over and over throughout both Testaments, the Bible relays this same story. When God repeats himself like this, the message he is conveying is extremely important. "Today when you hear his voice, do not harden your hearts . . ." (Heb 3:7–8). Every day is today.

Today means us.

St. John Paul II encouraged us,

> Brothers and sisters, do not be afraid to welcome Christ and accept his power . . . . Do not be afraid. Open, I say open wide the doors for Christ. Do not be afraid. Christ knows "that which is in man." He alone knows it. So often today, man does not know that which is in him, in the depths of his mind and heart. So often he is uncertain about the meaning of his life on this earth. He is assailed by doubt, a doubt which turns into despair. We ask you, therefore, we beg you with humility and with trust, let Christ speak to man. He alone has words of life, yes, of life eternal.[2]

Step-by-step through the scriptures, the Lord assured me that as he released me from my destructive habits, relationships, circumstances, and desires, I would find rest and peace, the milk and honey of my earthly Promised Land. Think of the extraordinary fruitfulness of the original land!

That's what I longed for. That's what I felt God promised. And that's what he delivered.

Facing Our Giants

This Promised Land is not without its giants, not for any of us. And yet God delivers them into our hands, too, if we will only trust through our fears. Freedom is a promise to each of us from God through Christ, and it's as close as the effort it takes to obtain it. I must only heed the warning of the scriptures to keep moving forward. Baby steps still move me ahead. When I cannot run, I need only crawl.

The Israelites left the slavery of sin and endured the aridity and deprivations of desert purification. They witnessed miraculous salvation and provision. Yet they refused the last battle: fear. To avoid making the same mistake, we must resist turning back out of fear of pain, failure, annihilation, being conquered, or the exhaustion of another battle, for,

> To whom did he swear that they should never enter his rest, but to those who are disobedient? So we see they were unable to enter because of unbelief. Therefore, while the promise of entering his rest remains, let us fear lest any of [us] be judged to have failed to reach it. For the good news comes to us just as to them; but the message which they heard did not benefit them, because it did not meet with faith in the hearers. (Heb 3:18–4:2)

Ultimately, our Promised Land is the beatific vision of heaven. But the good news of the Gospel is that it begins now, for "the kingdom of God is at hand" (Mk 1:15).

What if God guarantees he will unleash something new and fresh into your life if you invite him in? What if the result could be as fruitful as the Promised Land, an unleashed reward, deep sanctification, utter fulfillment, and abundant salvation? Please do not forfeit more of God out of fear. I beg you, do not be tempted to despair and forfeit the dream he planted within you, for with the promise you receive through persevering in faith, you also receive more of God.

An Invitation

As I opened my heart to the Holy Spirit's voice in the scriptures and his action in my life, I began to understand he had long been speaking, moving, and working through my patterns before I ever consciously discerned them. You are about to see how God is already actively working through your patterns too.

The Holy Spirit has been at work with great power since the beginning of time. The Bible shows us that God follows a certain pattern in the way he speaks to humanity generally, and you and me specifically. Knowing his methods helps us, like Jesus, discern where in our lives to look for his actions and how to hear his instructions.

After we investigate God's manner of unleashing, we're going to probe our own individual patterns of behavior. Have you ever wondered why you continue in the same destructive habits long after you should have learned better? We will investigate what sin *really* is, why we shouldn't sin, and how to eventually break destructive behavior habits.

Next, we'll take a thorough look at our relationships. Why do we seem to stay enslaved to the influence and opinion of that particular person? Why do we keep running into the same types of people over and over? Isn't that frustrating? They're so awful. We'll discover that they are mirrors in our lives to motivate us toward change and freedom, so that they—"O happy fault!"—actually become our spiritual allies.

Then we'll inspect our circumstances and the issues God might be addressing through those situations. We'll seek to determine the message God could be sending through our difficulties and catch a glimpse of the interior castle he is building with tender determination through our suffering.

After that we'll embrace our desires. *All* of them. Isn't that unusual? Decadent, maybe? Shining light on our desires can help remove the hidden power they often wield on our motivations and emotions.

We're going to survey exactly how to hear God speak directly to us on a daily basis. I'm going to share with you the specifics of how God led me through this entire process with the scriptures, so you can try it, too, if you like.

Finally, we're going to explore why the answer to prayer is always "fish," dry bones live, and the dead are raised when the Holy Spirit is invited and unleashed in our lives! I hope you're ready; we're about to begin discerning the patterns.

God Prompt

As we finish this chapter, the thought of striding toward that great Promised Land and of unleashing the power of the Spirit might seem a little unnerving. But don't be afraid. Remember that our loving God approaches us gently, with great tenderness. And it all begins with a single, simple step: by answering the question: "What do you wish?"

Imagine the Lord speaking those four plaintive words to you right now. What do you want to say to him?

> Jesus: (Insert your name), what do you wish?
> You: Lord, I wish . . .
>> But I am afraid of . . .
>> I believe; help my unbelief.

Are you ready to take this courageous step of faith? What would cause *anyone* to seek out such an encounter with the Lord? The answer, of course, is our desire to receive and experience everything the Holy Spirit wants to give us. When we open ourselves wide to the unleashed power of the Holy Spirit in our lives, we discover that we ourselves are unleashed from the patterns in our lives that create the most problems for us, the toxic habits, patterns, and relationships of our lives.

By turning to the scriptures and reading the Word of God, all the while expecting to hear from him and determined to obey, little by little we are freed from these soul-crushing burdens for truly unleashed living. In the chapters that follow, we'll find out how.

2

*W*ho Touched Me?

Mark 5:31

Unleashing the Holy Spirit's Power

The moment we invite the Holy Spirit into our lives and circumstances, we have touched him with faith. And nothing is as irresistible to God as faith. Faith moves him immediately to action.

Consider Jesus' question, put to a woman who had suffered a bleeding uterus for twelve humiliating years. Her hemorrhage made her unclean according to the Old Testament Law, unable to touch others or to be touched. How can that be, when God made a woman to bleed on a monthly basis? How could she help it? Why, then, was she ostracized, stigmatized, put away, seemingly abandoned by God?

Did she suffer in silence those many years? Maybe she was too depressed to care. Possibly she saw no conceivable help on the horizon after all the doctors repeatedly filled her heart with hope and her body with snake oil. They drained her of every penny, yet the very essence of her physical life continued to leave her body. Was she afraid? I bet so. I bet she was afraid of my judgment and gossip about her illness being a result of some personal sin. Anyone would reasonably decide this type of "female problem" was probably due to some sexual indiscretion, some perversion, or something else very untoward. She could never have kids, after all, and *that* was certainly God's holy finger in her face. Of course, right?

Perhaps she feared the condescension or indifference of those who shoved her unworthy self out of the way as they elbowed toward Jesus themselves.

Whatever the case, on this day she ventured from the security of home, and eyes downcast, pushed into the midst of a jostling, pressing crowd, put out a trembling hand, and touched the hem of his cloak.

He felt her faith unleash a miraculous, virtuous power from him, and he turned to her, full-faced, immediately. "Who touched me?"

Why does he ask her that question? Does he not know?

Notice, especially, that the woman's faith trumps her fear and causes her to act, and when she does, the power of God is unleashed in *her*. Once Jesus turns to her, he expects her to tell him the whole truth. She tells him everything: the anguish, the humiliation, the uncleanness, the secrets, the unfairness, the fear, the abandonment, and what she wished from him—the whole, ugly truth. "He said to her, 'Daughter, your faith has saved you. Go in peace and be cured of your affliction'" (Mk 5:34, NAB).

All I can say to that is, Alleluia!

As soon as we touch Jesus with faith and truth, he accepts our intention and gets right to work showing us how he has been active all along, mostly without our cooperation.

For her, it was an immediate and miraculous unleashing. But most often for us, it's not.

Don't we seem to waste a lot of time and energy trying to accomplish substantial change on our own, in our lives, and the lives of those we love, until we understand God's ways? Learning his methods helps me discern where to look for his actions, how to hear his instructions, and how to work *with* him.

> Therefore, as the Holy Spirit says, "Today, when you hear his voice, do not harden your hearts as in the rebellion, on the day of testing in the wilderness, where your fathers put me to the test and saw my works for forty years. Therefore I was provoked with that generation, and said, 'They always go astray in their hearts; *they have not known my ways.*'" (Heb 3:7–10, emphasis added)

The Holy Spirit has been at work unleashing his people since the beginning of time and has always worked in particular ways. The Bible shows us that God follows certain patterns in the way he speaks to and works in humanity generally, and you and me specifically. Do you think it's comforting that he wants us to know the pattern through which he works? According to the scriptures, when we know his patterns we are less likely to go astray in our hearts.

Expect God to Do Something

Our first clue to God's ways is in the leading burst of scripture, the Creation account in Genesis:

> The earth was without form and void, and darkness was upon the face of the deep; and the Spirit of God was moving over the face of the waters. And God said, "Let there be light"; and there was light. And God saw that the light was good; and

God separated the light from the darkness. (Gn
1:2–4)

As is frequently true in scripture, a lot of time is covered in
these few verses. The Spirit of God "was moving," meaning
brooding over or agitating the waters, preparing the depths
for his action. In the original language, the term *light* can also
mean happiness, and *darkness* can mean misery, sorrow, or
wickedness. God creates light and happiness where there
is chaos and sorrow. What an incredible hope and promise.

This opening offering contains a wonderful principle
that helps carry me through difficult, tumultuous times:
God *will* act; he unleashes light and life; he orders what is
disordered; and he can make something out of nothing!
"Scripture bears witness to faith in creation 'out of nothing' as a truth full of promise and hope" (CCC 297). When
I am completely at a loss as to how I should proceed in a
circumstance or have not the resources to move forward, I
can always count on the Holy Spirit, the Way Maker, to do
something. Predictably unpredictable, we never know the
details of when to expect him, just that we *should* expect
him, because he *will* arrive.

When the Holy Spirit is unleashed, incredible things
always happen. Things grow luminous, structured, alive.

In the first chapters of Genesis, we watch as God painstakingly prepares a dazzling, diverse home for mankind.
Isn't he neighborly? Generous? He gives what he has, wel-
comes the other, and opens himself to surprise, even dread-
ful surprise.

We know the story: our first parents sinned and chaos
followed. The order of their relationship to God, to one
another, and even the earth itself and the animal kingdom,
all fell into tragedy and disorder. Is there anything in your
life that feels chaotic and confusing? Has anything been
wasted or ruined? I pray you will hold the matter in your
heart and open it fully to the Holy Spirit, for his tendency

to act is so strong, it even includes what has fallen into ruin through sin.

Grace Superabounds

When I was little, I watched the *Little House on the Prairie* episode in which Mary went blind because of scarlet fever. After that, I would sometimes pretend I was blind and try to move through my house. I discovered how very familiar things could suddenly become frighteningly unfamiliar. The Eden account teaches us that sin introduces a lack of order that leads to unfamiliarity, chaos, and misery. The whole story of history, in fact, chronicles what happens when sin prevails. We might even call this chaos and sorrow *darkness*.

Sometimes, what we know God can do and what we believe God will do are two different things. I always knew God *could* bring structure to my disorder, but because the disorder in my life was almost always my own doing (sin or rebellion), I didn't believe he *would*.

Have you experienced this doubt?

"O truly necessary sin of Adam, destroyed completely by the Death of Christ! O happy fault that earned for us so great, so glorious a Redeemer!" (Paschal Vigil Mass Exsultet).

St. Paul puts it even more succinctly: "where sin increased, grace abounded all the more" (Rom 5:20). In essence St. Paul is saying that grace *superabounds* wherever sin abounds.

The grace of Christ surpasses the grace we lost, both in time and history, and in our own lives. Why? The Holy Spirit's nature is one of action. He must act. And so, he does. Alleluia! But only in the "fullness of time" (Gal 4:4, NAB).

Welcome a Slow Unleashing

Like a child jumping around in the backseat on a long trip, I remember asking the Lord frequently, "Are we there yet?" I have a slip of paper on my desk from a meditation around that time years ago that says, "The bigger the oak, the deeper the roots." Indeed.

The first homily in the world was preached at Creation, a demonstration of flawless law, flawless plan, flawless arrangement, and flawless method. Six days of labor rigorously planned, scheduled, and completed, followed by rest. Even now, doesn't the cosmos remain a divine protest against hurry?

Nature never hurries. Every area of her operation illustrates plan, peace, and unhurried responsibility. Hurry implies confusion, impatience of slow growth, and lack of a definite procedure. How often do I mistake ambition for inspiration and seek to make energy a substitute for a clearly defined intention?

Peace is the poise of a great Nature in harmony with himself who only does wondrous things (Ps 72:18). The greater, higher, and nobler his work, the slower is its growth, and the more lasting its success. His work is always centered, reliable, and controlled.

The eternal soul is the highest order of nature, his most majestic effort, and so it must be the product of steady, deliberate growth. Trust the delicacy of a slow unleashing. Welcome it if it must be slow, knowing the results are certain, as you might accept the dark weight of winter with absolute assurance that it will surely submit to a bright and gentle spring.

The Spirit's in the Details

I'll never forget how the Lord startled me with a transforming invitation, even while I was hard at work in ministry. I had meticulously planned our church's Vacation Bible School. Because my pride was involved and I had a reputation to uphold, it simply had to be over-the-top awesome because every year had to be more incredible than the last. I recruited artists and musicians and directed a decoration scheme worthy of Broadway. That Vacation Bible School was incredible.

We repurposed entire sections of the sanctuary. The sound booth became a castle, complete with ramparts, and the cardboard I had painted and fastened so carefully pulled the paint off when we removed it. Being Mrs. Responsible and proud of it, I decided I must repaint. But not just repaint— I also had to fill in the teeny tiny dots left behind by popped paint bubbles from a hurried roller brush. Utterly exhausted and angry that no one was there to help me do it, I was daubing paint on the wall with a three-haired detail brush (I kid you not) when I felt the Holy Spirit gently ask, "Sonja, what are you doing?"

Almost like the prodigal son who came to himself in the pigpen, I found myself wondering, *What* am *I doing?* I had spent an entire month, forty or fifty hours every week, working—overworking, truth be told—on that Vacation Bible School. We had reached hundreds of kids, and yet, in my mind, my job wasn't done until I had repainted a wall that had been defaced through my campaign. And not just repainted, but *painstakingly* refurbished with a detail brush to fill in holes that were only detectable upon magnified examination.

And that is why I was still there in that sanctuary long after everyone else had gone, resenting it all, and screaming at my toddler to be quiet through his nap time while I finished.

That gentle question made me stop for a moment to consider again what I was doing and why. Most of my frustration as one who earnestly desired my own unleashing and that of those I loved was from well-meant but misguided efforts. Assuming I knew the proper way to direct myself and those around me, I went about making it happen. Only it never happened. Matters only got worse. My obsessive perfectionism spilled over into so many areas of my life, and until the Holy Spirit laid that question on my heart, so gently, so deliberately, I never saw that it was obsessive perfectionism, or how pervasive and unrealistic it was.

What the Holy Spirit invited me to consider is that no one cared about the obsessive details but me; they didn't matter. Furthermore, my perfectionist tendencies were actually working against me and my family, and against my relationship with God.

Although the Holy Spirit definitely worked through the efforts of our team for that Vacation Bible School, he most certainly did not demand that I repaint the invisible dots on the sound booth. Why? Because the Holy Spirit never forces; he invites. Aren't compulsions simply force in disguise?

I read *The Lion, the Witch and the Wardrobe* when I was about eight years old. In the book, C. S. Lewis portrays God as a lion. Because I was so young, I did not remember much about the story, but what I did remember stayed with me, mysteriously, all the way into adulthood until I saw the movie and was startled by the quote. It was one sentence: "Of course he isn't safe. But he is good!"[1]

Jesus teaches us that force, manipulation, and pushing are all hallmarks of Satan's activity and influence. The Holy Spirit asked me to consider my impatient perfectionism as an attempt to force myself and others, and invited me with a mere gentle question to explore all the possible answers: "What are you doing, Dear One?"

Because he is persistently unleashing his matchless power, we may assume it must involve hurry, pushing, or force. On the contrary, "he will not break a bruised reed or quench a smoldering wick" (Mt 12:20). While he could break me like a hollow stick and one already bent, he will not do it. Instead, he is tender with the spiritually weak and gentle with the soul in which divine light is flickering out. "Nothing is so strong as gentleness, nothing so gentle as real strength," wrote St. Francis de Sales.[2]

Freed from the Darkness

Answering and acting on Jesus' question "What do you wish?" touches him with faith, unleashing truth and the Holy Spirit's terrifying gentleness into the darkness of our lives. Because we often find that our behaviors, circumstances, and relationships seem veiled in impenetrable darkness, we must also probe exactly what causes God's order and clarity to enter into those specific day-to-day things that have somehow become disordered, so we can know where to look for help and light in our own circumstances and feelings of darkness. The scriptures tell us where to look.

> In many and various ways God spoke of old to our fathers by the prophets; but in these last days he has spoken to us by a Son, whom he appointed the heir of all things, through whom also he created the world. He reflects the glory of God and bears the very stamp of his nature, upholding the universe by his word of power. (Heb 1:1–3)

This passage gives me chills. Jesus was the One through whom creation was spoken into existence and the One through whom it is held that way now. I had a hard time, once, reconciling a thundering, lightning, hailing, punishing God with a gentle Jesus. Yet we see here that he is the

image and face of the terrifyingly gentle, invisible God; "in
him all things were created, in heaven and on earth, visible
and invisible, whether thrones or dominions or principali-
ties or authorities—all things were created through him and
for him. He is before all things, and in him all things hold
together" (Col 1:16–17).

Remember "God said," and light was unleashed in
the first Creation? In the New Testament, God is sending
light again.

> In the beginning was the Word, and the Word
> was with God, and the Word was God. He was
> in the beginning with God; all things were made
> through him, and without him was not anything
> made that was made. In him was life, and the
> life was the light of men. The light shines in the
> darkness, and the darkness has not overcome it."
> (Jn 1:1–5)

Like the Big Bang that leisurely coalesced into spectacu-
larly vivid nebulae and the diversity of our life-supporting
planet, according to St. John's first chapter God unleashed
light once again at the Incarnation—a new, transforming,
spiritual light into a world enshrouded in spiritual darkness.
John uses two important designations for what will ultimately become, throughout this passage, a vivid description
of the Christ—Word and Light.

"God said" there should be light, and light exploded
beautifully into the cosmos in Genesis 1. In a way very similar to the first creation, in the "fullness of time" (Gal 4:4,
NAB), he unleashed a spiritual light that began a new creation, a redemption, a reordering of all that had fallen and
was in disrepair. Brooding and agitating over her, readying
her for the unleashing of life, he "overshadowed" the new
Eve and brought forth a new Adam. Together, they began
the rewinding of time. How was this "new creation" accomplished? Through the Word:

> What came to be through him was life,
> And this life was the light of the human race;
> The light shines in the darkness,
> And the darkness has not overcome it. (Jn 1:3–5,
> NAB)

As we read in the *Catechism of the Catholic Church*, the Light and Word are the person of Jesus.

> Through all the words of Sacred Scripture, God speaks only one single Word, his one Utterance in whom he expresses himself completely: For this reason, the Church has always venerated the Scriptures as she venerates the Lord's Body. She never ceases to present to the faithful the bread of life, taken from the one table of God's Word and Christ's Body. (CCC 102–104)

How do I release the Holy Spirit's light in my life? How do I steadily and clearly hear him speak to me personally about my behavior, circumstances, relationships, and desires? How will I truly know myself and the real motives behind my actions? "For the word of God is living and active, sharper than any two-edged sword, piercing to the division of soul and spirit, of joints and marrow, and discerning the thoughts and intentions of the heart" (Heb 4:12).

If the scriptures are that powerful, how will I ever become unleashed from all that binds me from abundant, joyful living and keeps me mired in toxic, unhealthy relationships and habits if I do not read and study them? (Specific ways to incorporate the scriptures into our daily diet are in chapter seven.)

> In Sacred Scripture, the Church constantly finds her nourishment and her strength, for she welcomes it not as a human word, "but as what it really is, the word of God." In the sacred books,

the Father who is in heaven comes lovingly to
meet his children, and talks with them. (CCC 104)

Once we expect his action and are listening for his voice in
the scriptures, he gets right to work unleashing. What is it
that the living, discerning scriptures accomplish that is so
powerful in the hands of the Holy Spirit? Truth.

Peeling Truth from the Outside, In

In one of my favorite, hopeful chapters of scripture, John 8,
Jesus tells us the secret to being unleashed for all those with
faith: "Jesus then said to the Jews who had believed in him,
'If you continue in my word, you are truly my disciples,
and you will know the truth, and the truth will make you
free'" (Jn 8:31–32). When we know and obey his teachings,
we continue in his Word. When we continue in his Word,
we are true disciples. True disciples know the truth, and
they are set free. The phrase *make you free* literally means
"loosed." *Unleashed.*

Jesus is saying my preconceptions, lack of introspection, destructive relationships, bad habits, hurtful events,
and disordered desires are enslaving me. In essence he says,
"I will tell you the truth, and you will be unleashed." Freedom is the ultimate reality. In the words of Simone Weil in
Gravity and Grace, "Truth is sought not because it is truth but
because it is good."[3]

There is a lovely consistency in the scriptures in how
the Holy Spirit works in our behaviors, circumstances, relationships, and desires. Because God knows and understands
that they are often rooted in childhood coping mechanisms,
he begins addressing our behaviors like one peels an onion:
working from the outside, steadily toward the inside in
deeper and deeper ways.

People who read the Bible often question me about
why God seems so brutal and exacting in the Old Testament,

where he ordered the total annihilation of entire cities, nations, people groups, and civilizations—men, women, children, property, and animals. They have trouble reconciling the Old Testament God with a tender, child-blessing, forgiveness-teaching Jesus; they feel the Testaments seem to be at odds with one another.

The Bible, and salvation history contained therein, however, is laid out a little like the onion metaphor—outward to inward. Old Testament scholars tell us God is probing and correcting the literal, visible, outward behavior of his infant people in the Old Testament. He is very strict, and the punishments are quick and sure, and even seem harsh at times. But the Old Testament lessons are those of children. God's Old Testament people came from the polytheism of Egypt, had no idea what worshipping one God meant, and did not have the indwelling power of the Holy Spirit to help them recognize or live up to the deeper standard of grace. They were spiritual children. With children, boundaries must be very tight and the consequences quick and obvious; this is to ensure their safety and to prepare them to think and work more deeply when their development is ready for it.

In the same way, the Church teaches that God provided outward behaviors and boundaries through the Law that would keep his Old Testament children safe and teach them to properly worship the One, True God, until he could lead them to the advent of the New Testament Messiah. At that point he could move to deeper truths, inward behaviors, with a truly upward, heavenly momentum. Because the outward man had been tutored throughout Old Testament history, God could begin probing and correcting the spiritual, invisible, inward behavior of his more mature New Testament people at the proper time.

When history and the people of God had matured and developed enough to handle deeper truths, he was faithful to reveal the fullness of himself through Christ, and the deeper, spiritual reality that he *is*. The spiritual depth of truth, reality, and life are the standard to which I am called by grace: "You shall be holy, for I am holy" (1 Pt 1:16). By grace, we can be holy. We can attain, experience, and communicate unleashed life—the life of God himself that he longs to share with us. Incredible!

The principle is: outward to inward. The Old Testament addressed the outside. Outward concerns behavior. The New Testament addresses the interior soul as well as the outward behavior. Inward includes our interior perceptions and beliefs, the real motivations underneath our outward behaviors. Just like our scriptural ancestors, the Holy Spirit began telling me the truth through the scriptures about my outward behaviors and then moved steadily more interiorly.

An Upward Spiral

Here's another way to look at it: My grandfather used to peel apples with his pocket-knife. He would start at the bottom and work his way up; around and around the apple he would go, very slowly, in order to offer me one unbroken peel. God works a little like this also. An upward-directed spiral leading straight into his arms.

St. Teresa of Avila's *The Interior Castle*, St. John of the Cross's *Ascent of Mount Carmel*, James Fowler's *Stages of Faith*, and Fr. Garrigou Lagrange's *The Three Ages of the Interior Life* all describe the paradox of the Holy Spirit's simultaneously outward-to-inward and upward spiral action. Once again, the Old Testament children of Israel illustrate the same.

When we study the 200-mile journey of the children of Israel from the slavery of Egypt to the land he promised, we discover this interesting (although possibly frustrating) principle in the most literal way. God's poor family's week-long journey turned into a forty-year marathon. They went around Mt. Sinai over and over and over for forty years. Granted, "forty years" in scriptural terms simply means something like "however long it took, it was the right amount of time." But the scriptures convey that however long it was, it was long enough for a doubting generation to be replaced by one that dared.

Not just once, but throughout their history, God's children repeatedly found themselves under the control of one kingdom or another. After Egypt, there was Assyria and Babylon, and later, Rome.

For us, too, the principle is the same as my grandfather's apple peel: throughout our lives and circumstances, we travel around and around the mountain of our predominant fault in an upward spiral to God. However, we are not covering the same ground over and over: The Holy Spirit is carefully economical with time and resources, and the human soul is a most valuable treasure. Instead, we move upward toward him in very small, gentle degrees with every revolution.

Desert Ways

Not only is the Holy Spirit unleashed in predictable ways, but he also works in predictable seasons. The children of Israel's example shows us that one of God's most predictable patterns is his desert "ways." The Holy Spirit is unleashed most powerfully in the lonely aridity of the desert. In fact, there is no biblical person of heroic faith and no saint I have ever studied who did not spend a significant amount of time in the desert.

In a scriptural sense, the desert is a paradox. A metaphor for both life and death, the desert can be a place of hopelessness or one of purposeful contemplation and prayer. Every desert season is either a time to detach from the world and surrender to God or one in which we yearn for the comforts of the world and yield to the flesh. Necessarily, the desert is empty and comfortless: Water and food, consolations, are scarce. There is no comfort from the battering wind and heat of day, nor the unfiltered cold of night. The dunes seem unending and are stark and lonely. But the desert is actually God's primary training ground. It is in the desert that you can be most effectively unleashed; you should cling to this promise when you find yourself there.

The most powerful experiences of God recorded in the scriptures almost always happen in the desert. If I can rest in the discomfort long enough for it to do its work of detachment, might I experience God more powerfully than ever before? The children of Israel teach us that the desert can be a barren place of great temptation. But from Jesus we learn the desert can also be a place of purposeful isolation, removal of distractions, calling and mission, and great graces.

The enemy uses the desert to tempt us to focus on scarcity. Satan lures us to the desert to weaken us and lead us to comfort-seeking sin and death. The Holy Spirit leads us to the desert to deeply strengthen and unleash us from what binds. In God's plan, the desert is a time to engage in ascetical practices. Unfortunately, GPS does not work in the desert, but used wisely, the blindness of the desert will be a time of preparation for what waits just beyond our desert experience.

Let's Review

Let's review God's ways and patterns of unleashing his Spirit:

God's Spirit is freedom. His first pattern is his nature to order and reorder even (and especially) those things that have fallen into ruin through sin. Like the woman with the hemorrhage who touched Jesus, we should always expect him to do something when we express to him the whole truth of what we wish for and take a step of active faith.

The Holy Spirit works slowly and carefully. He does not force; he works with (not despite) our development, temperaments, personalities, relationships, circumstances, and desires.

He unleashes and works through the Word. The Eucharist and the scriptures are truth and light for our disordered and ruined habits, relationships, and circumstances.

The Holy Spirit works outward to inward, and in an upward spiral to God.

God works most deeply in desert times.

An Invitation

Haven't you had habits, experiences, relationships, and desires to which you wanted to respond based on your own experiences or your own wisdom? I have learned that such an approach gets me in trouble and usually does not produce the change I want or expect, because my way almost always involves forcing or hurry. Additionally, the problems I face in my life may be overwhelming and multiple. What do I work on first?

This has become my guideline: Jesus is my way; I do not need a map; I will look to see where the Father is at work and join him there. I watch to see what the Father is already doing by examining my patterns. I do nothing in a hurry or on my own initiative, as Jesus does nothing in a hurry or on his initiative. Because the Father loves me, he shows me what he is doing and invites me to join him.

And so, take a moment to invite the Lord to show you the map of your life. Invite him to show you where he is at work, and trust that he will speak gently and steadily through the scriptures. Even if he leads us to experience painful, lonely desert times, we can have faith that when we cooperate with him, it will be productive rather than simply hurtful.

God Prompt

The next steps of your journey will entail your listening closely to the promptings of your own heart and taking notice of what God is trying to say to you. You may want to flip back to the first page and read the chapter again, this time noticing the places that caused a strong reaction of some kind—perhaps longing, perhaps anxiety, perhaps a flash of insight.

What was the most significant sentence, idea, or paragraph you read in this chapter? If you are amenable to making marks in your books, I hope you will mark sentences or sections that stand out for you in some way. I often draw light bulbs next to important sentences or ideas in books I am reading. Because he wills it, right now God is working all around me and my life. I long to experience him but often fail to realize that I am experiencing God day after day, because I simply have not learned how to recognize his ways. If anything particularly struck you in this chapter, could it be the voice of God, already acting and moving in your heart and life?

Attempt to discern the pattern: Can I use the principles ("Let's Review" points,) from this chapter to identify an area, pattern, or circumstance in which God is already at work in my life?

Attempt to hear him speak through the Word: How will I know what to do? Where do I start? As you repeat the following verse in his presence, please emphasize each word or phrase in turn. Ask him to speak to your heart very clearly through this verse. You might try it like this:

> "*Lord*, we do not know where you are going; how
> can we know the way?" Jesus said to him,

"I am the way, and the truth, and the life . . ." (Jn 14:5–6)

"Lord, *we* do not know where you are going; how can we know the way?" Jesus said to him, "I am the way, and the truth, and the life . . ." (Jn 14:5–6).

"Lord, we *do not know* where you are going; how can we know the way?" Jesus said to him, "I am the way, and the truth, and the life . . ." (Jn 14:5–6)

"Lord, we do not know *where* you are going; how can we know the way?" Jesus said to him, "I am the way, and the truth, and the life . . ." (Jn 14:5–6)

"Lord, we do not know where *you* are going; how can we know the way?" Jesus said to him, "I am the way, and the truth, and the life . . ." (Jn 14:5–6)

Continue emphasizing each word or phrase in turn until you have focused on them all. What has God said to you through this verse?

Now that we know something about how to unleash the Holy Spirit in our lives so that we can be unleashed, I hope you're ready; we're about to discover what it means to be unleashed.

3

$\mathcal{H}$as No One Condemned You?

Reframing Your Story

She is startlingly beautiful under the grime, wisps of dark hair fluttering in the hot wind and sticking in the dusty sweat on her temples. She keeps her gaze averted to hide her fear and pain as betrayal lashes at her from all sides. Her dress is inside out, untied at the nape, and it rips as she jerks, first to one side, then the other, against the painful grip of the men dragging her, stumbling, through the crowded street to stand before Jesus. They are dirty voyeurs; she has recent, intimate knowledge of one of them.

"Adulteress," the guardians of morality charge, when they reach Jesus. "Caught in the act." Murmurs and knowing glances of derision roll through the righteous crowd. Jesus looks her in the eye, and her initial defiance and bluster disappear like a deflating balloon in a wash of humiliation.

41

Everyone present knows adultery is a capital crime. Some
are already holding stones. But who caught her? And why?
Who and where is her lover?

Having witnessed it once, she knows only too well
what is in store for her: a screaming mob meticulously
selects jagged, grapefruit-sized rocks and heaves them at a
human body huddled protectively in the dirt, bludgeoning
the breath and blood from her body, bit by bit, until she is
dead.

Only one thing can save her now: for a person to be
put to death, the Law requires that there be at least two
eyewitnesses—eyewitnesses to the very act of adultery.

How do they know she is an adulteress? Did they peer
through her curtains to witness the stolen tryst? And how
much had they seen? Were their hearts not filled with adultery as they watched? When they had seen enough, did they
storm the door of her bedroom where she lay naked and vulnerable? Did she struggle in fear, like a squalling cat being
forced into a sack and hauled to the river, as they wrestled
to push her, carelessly, into recently discarded garments?

Her lover, now nowhere to be seen, must have been in
on the plot. In any case it is not really the woman they want
to expose, but the Law they are zealous to uphold. She is
simply a pawn, a means to lure Jesus into a death trap of
his own. Will he take the side of the sinner, as he so often
seemed to do, and free her and forsake the Law he claims
to preach? Or will he condemn her to the death she surely
deserves?

They can barely contain their bloodlust. They are sick
of his adoring crowds, his flocks of dirty sinners. They
deeply resent his scathing criticism, his usurping of their
authority. "What do you say?" they demand of him.

How shocked they are when Jesus completely ignores
both challenge and drama. Strangely, he stoops down to
gather his thoughts. Silence rises like a thick fog when he

reaches down and scribbles in the dirt, like the finger that printed the Law in stone on Sinai millennia before.

Everyone cranes his neck to decipher the mysterious words. What does he write? Only they will ever know. Whatever it is, it escapes them. They press for an answer.

At last he stands. "If any one of you is without sin, let him be the first to throw a stone at her."

A gasp or two, an extended silence as every person present is made to know their personal sins, and one by one the stones thud to the ground. Slowly, the men shuffle away, starting with the oldest. Perhaps he is the wisest. Maybe he is most guilty.

How did she feel in that moment, alone with Jesus among the stones meant to crush the life out of her? Was she terrified for a different reason now? Was she able to look at him at all?

"Has no one condemned you?"

"No one, Lord," she whispers through trembling lips. He speaks again, this time to unleash her and reframe her story forever. And the only one qualified to condemn her, doesn't.

Words of truth, from Truth himself: "Neither do I condemn you; go, and do not sin again" (Jn 8:11).

Go, and Do Not Sin Again

As I walked in the door, my eyes fell on the pink envelope sitting on top of the afternoon mail. Two shocking things immediately made my heart pound: The handwriting on the envelope was my father's. And my husband had already opened the envelope and read the card.

Infuriated, I screamed at the man I married, demanding an explanation. How dare he presume to be the first to see the only words my father had offered me in three years—the entire length of our marriage? My father had not walked me down the aisle or danced at our wedding. I could not listen to "Butterfly Kisses" on the radio without a physical reaction.

My father had always been an authoritarian, demanding unquestioning and instant submission. Years later, when Dad received an invitation to our marriage, he promptly called me and insisted I move the date. It was too soon, he said. I was too young. I refused, not out of stubbornness (well, maybe partly), but because my husband and I were cohabitating at the time. I knew living together was wrong, and I wanted to end the situation as soon as possible. When I wouldn't budge, Dad summoned me to his house for a "discussion."

I knew it was pointless to go; I had been down that road with him many times before and knew any "discussion" would consist solely of him demanding I do what he wanted. I went anyway, because I was afraid not to.

Sure enough, we had words. The confrontation between my father and me grew heated. I am not proud of flipping him the bird as I left with him chasing me out the door and down the driveway repeating, "You'd better be sure this is what you want!"

We hadn't spoken to one another since.

Then I got the pink birthday card in the mail in my father's handwriting. Seeing that little well-wish reopened all my old wounds—deep, intimate wounds that my husband's insensitivity had rubbed salt into. Maybe he had acted out of a sincere desire to protect me, but I felt violated, controlled, and betrayed.

I flew into the hottest rage of my whole life. Before that, I had gotten into physical and verbal combat with other girls in high school and college, and a fiancé. Later, anger provoked me to punch holes in the walls of my home, destroy dishes, burn rubber till the tires were bald, and break locks and doors, and once, a remote control. But I had never blacked out with rage before that day. I remember physically attacking my husband and him holding my wrists so I couldn't hit him. I kicked instead, very proud that I could writhe out of his grasp enough to hurt him, a man at least twice my size and weight.

When it was over I realized I couldn't remember most of what had happened, and I was deeply ashamed of my behavior. I remember asking God, "What in the world is wrong with me?" At the time I was reading one chapter of Proverbs every day. As I began to read the scripture passage for the next morning, my eyes fell on the verse that was the answer to my question:

> Like a dog that returns to his vomit
> is a fool that repeats his folly. (Prv 26:11)

Don't you love the pithiness of the Bible? A short time later I found another insight: "Be angry and sin not" (Ps 4:4). God used these two verses to confront me about my behavior pattern of rage. Not anger, Dear One. Rage.

Each time I spewed my anger out to the Lord in prayer (for I was frequently offended and angry), he spoke to my heart, quietly and persistently leading me to recall times I had been destructively, aggressively, sinfully angry. As I began to reflect on these memories, he pointed out that my pattern of rage emerged when I was criticized by men who were in positions of authority over me, especially those with aggressive leadership styles. I knew God wanted me to change this pattern, and I struggled to understand how it was possible. I had no idea why I was doing what I was doing. Was this rage even my fault? I often justified my outbursts readily, saying, "Everyone would be perfectly fine if they just didn't make me mad!"

Breaking the Cycle of Sin

I reached a turning point when I began to notice a disturbing tendency of parental aggression toward my first son, who was a baby at the time. I grew terrified. More than anything on earth, I feared making my kids feel powerless and worthless like I had often felt as a child. I recognized that unless I got a grip on my destructive behavior, I was destined to repeat it with my kids. I resolved to change this family pattern, and I begged God to help me. "How do I break through and get on?"

These kinds of family patterns are found in many families; in fact, they're in every biblical family except the Holy Family. Some theologians call this type of sin a *predominant fault.*

> It is of primary importance that we recognize our predominant fault and have no illusions about it. This is so much the more necessary as our adversary, the enemy of our soul, knows it quite well and makes use of it to stir up trouble in and about us. . . . The predominant fault is the weak spot. . . . The enemy of souls seeks exactly this easily vulnerable point in each one, and he finds it without difficulty. Therefore we must recognize it also.[1]

As we've already established, whatever else it is, our predominant fault is primarily *sin.* One of the distinct difficulties we often have in understanding how to live well the Christian life is a clear knowledge of *sin:* what it is, why we shouldn't, and why we should care. In my travels and exchanges with others at conferences and events, I have discovered that people typically view sin as dos and don'ts; we rationalize it as something we know we shouldn't participate in but that is too small to matter: a white lie, a pad of sticky notes brought home from the office, driving ten miles over the speed limit.

Growing up, I understood sin to be a failed attempt to hit a perfect bull's-eye, a miss that angers God—or that life is like a white board, and every sin is a dirty ink mark. I imagined a standard of perfection that everyone must individually strive to attain, realizing all along that we can never, and will never, come close to reaching it. Each miss earns us a mark until the white scoreboard of our lives is black with sin marks. Jesus comes along with his forgiveness eraser and wipes all our messy marks away through Baptism and Confession. Beyond this, sin seems to have no importance for us at all.

I confess I have a bit of a rebellious streak. For a long time I just didn't see what the big deal was about sin (as long as I confessed, just to be safe). Who cares if we've missed the mark a few times, or are a little dirty? No one is perfect. Heaven is a long time away—practical only for the elderly, the sick, and those who are conservative enough buy other forms of life insurance. So aside from death, which is in all likelihood years away, why should I worry about sin at all?

Let's look at it another way: Part of the literal meaning of the word *sin* is to forfeit. What might I be giving up if I continue in sin? Sure, if I continue in mortal sin (1 Jn 5:14–17), I put my soul at risk. I could even forfeit eternal life. But most of us never think about how much those little sins get us off track; heaven seems far, far away—nothing we need to worry about right now, we think.

Actually, however, sin has *everything* to do with the quality of my life *right now*. "The thief comes only to steal and kill and destroy; I came that they may have life, and have it abundantly" (Jn 10:10). The thief, the enemy, comes to us to destroy us, but Jesus comes to us to give us *abundant life*: exponentially multiplying, hyperabundant, superexcessive, exceedingly superfluous, vehemently superior, unleashed *life*.

Alleluia! This superabundance is God's eternal life, and he wants to share that with us *right now*. His being. His aliveness. His unleashing. Not a quantity of days, since God is not of time, but their quality. He gives us a share in his own superabundant life. "Faith makes us taste in advance the light of the beatific vision, the goal of our journey here below. Then we shall see God 'face to face', 'as he is.' So faith is already the beginning of eternal life" (CCC 163). I don't know about you, but I don't want to purposely forfeit abundant life ever, ever, ever again. Abundant life is how I want to live *every* day.

Breaking the Power of Your Fault

Abundant life is what my predominant fault detracts from my soul. Every single sin, major or minor, leeches some life away, "for the wages of sin is death . . ." (Rom 6:23). Satan would like to lead us through our predominant fault, straight into complete and utter annihilation.

Several years ago I was shocked by an invitation to give a eulogy at a funeral. I had just come into full communion with the Church, and for over a year my relationship with my husband was extremely strained because of that. I had also recently given birth to my second child and taken a salaried job to which God had led me and prepared me for years to do. But now, preparing to speak at that funeral, I had to come to terms with another simple fact: not everyone agreed that I was the best person for the job. A beloved seminarian and the surviving spouse's best friend had done the job together as volunteers for years; both had been passed over in order for me to get it.

I was elated to get the job, but it felt as if the entire community believed I had usurped the best friend (and probably gotten it through dubious means). I was maligned, persecuted, and even stalked until I was forced to report to my bishop and take legal action. My relationship with the widow, her best friend, and most of that community was particularly strained and difficult at a time when my marriage and hormones also left me feeling pushed to the limit.

I had no idea why the individual had asked me to speak at such a painful time and place, and guessed the invitation was meant as a peace offering. I deeply desired to be respectful and sensitive to the grief of everyone present, as well as the emotions of all who were involved in the conflict, and was touched by what I assumed was a gesture of good will.

I accepted the olive branch and labored over what to say, worrying and praying about it constantly until the evening came (it helped that I had a genuine affection for the deceased). Afterward, the priest praised the eulogy and joked that he wanted me to speak for him when he died; I was relieved to the point of tears.

When I returned home that night, exhausted by all the emotion and tension, my husband asked me how it went. Since I had no idea how it went, I told him I felt pretty good about it and that the priest had praised my speech. My husband replied, "I can't believe you would be proud of a talk you gave at someone's funeral."

I was devastated. Then I got pissed. But at that point in my journey with God, I had left aggressive rages behind. Instead, I seethed for days. And as I did, a particular scripture passage seemed to come up repeatedly in my prayer time, in Bible study, on the radio—everywhere!

> Each person is tempted when he is lured and
> enticed by his own desire. Then desire when it
> has conceived gives birth to sin; and sin when it
> is full-grown brings forth death. (Jas 1:14–15)

"What are you trying to tell me, God?" I demanded. "Am I guilty of pride after all?"

Shortly after my husband's accusation, I had a disturbing dream. I was in an abandoned cinema with a male friend. We were running through the cinema, away from a two-story-tall vampire bat. We raced through set after set of double metal doors into one dark and empty theater after another, our hurried steps echoing around us, but the enormous hissing bat was always close behind. Eventually I sprinted through a final set of doors, but my friend did not make it. As I looked over my shoulder through the closing door, I was horrified to see the vampire bat devour my dear friend. Abruptly, the dream ended, but it was so vivid and disturbing I remembered it in detail.

Could it mean anything? Who was the friend, and why was he destroyed? As I prayed and asked the Lord to show me what it all meant, eventually he led me to understand that the friend was my husband: my anger was devouring both him and our marriage.

Hot, grateful tears spring to my eyes as I write those words, because I had never before realized how destructive my silent, seething anger could be to the people in close proximity to me. I was cut to the heart, determined to keep working on my ugly predominant monster. I became willing to investigate the roots of my anger more deeply.

Because the "wages of sin is death," sin always leaves destruction in its wake (Rom 6:23). That screaming fight I had with my spouse? My children witnessed every ugly glare and snarled word; invisible wounds are difficult to heal. That glass of wine that turned into three or four? Its moments of release left sharp words and embarrassing actions in their wake. That pair of shoes I bought on credit? The brief rush it gave me to have something new left its debt to surprise me on the statement.

Jesus said it this way, "Everyone who commits sin is a slave to sin" (Jn 8:34). Satan would love nothing better than for our sin to turn into a practice, our practice to turn into a habit, our habit to turn into a stronghold, and our stronghold to turn into slavery—a compulsion that leads us and those around us straight to hell. Can you see now why we should never sin?

What was so difficult for me to realize is that sin does not only include actions. In fact the actual definition includes mistakes, guilt, untruth, unreality, lack, fault, and harm. This truth is why, in part, we say in the Confiteor at Mass, "I confess that I have sinned . . . in what I have done, and what I have failed to do . . ." My behaviors are simply the first layer of the onion, the first pattern that God addresses. Sin also includes my erroneous perceptions. What do I mean? Offenses. Prejudice. Unforgiveness. Hypersensitivity. One of my theology professors wrote this equation on the board in class, and I have never forgotten it:

$$S + P = B$$
Situation + Perception = Behavior

What I *think* about a situation dictates how I will act. When my perception of the situation has been reframed, my behavior can change.

Situation: Once I was able to discern that my seething anger at my husband's unfairness was fueled by a deep fear of criticism, it was revealed to be an irrational reaction, proud in and of itself. (Am I somehow above criticism?)

Perception: Once I saw my anger as irrational, I was no longer so angry.

Behavior: After I was no longer raging inside, I was able to express my hurt to the Lord and allow him to correct it in his presence without acting out.

The Holy Spirit invited me to look at my behavior patterns so I might discern my predominant fault. I needed to know my predominant fault particularly so I could begin thinking about it differently, so that my behavior could change for the better.

Outward, Then Inward

Remember the principle of outward to inward, and upward spiral to God? Outward concerns behavior. Inward spiritual work includes our interior perceptions and beliefs, the real motivations underneath our outward behaviors. According to the science of psychology, inward work on behaviors often means some examination of the past.

I am sometimes met by derision in people who feel any consideration of past events and circumstances, especially from childhood, is useless rehashing. After all, it is so much easier to leave all that alone. The past is sometimes painful. We might cry, and we hate to cry. If you're like me, you might have even sworn never to cry another tear. Many of us flee from our beginnings as far and as quickly as we can, because we sense we might be swallowed up by the damage or the danger.

Isn't there a difference, however, in moving beyond my past and an outright rejection of important aspects of who I am? We should live in the present, absolutely, but science has taught us a thorough understanding of the present requires some understanding of our early formation because all our perceptions and habits and behaviors are rooted there. It's unhealthy to run from the past, because it is the root of the soul, and one cannot dismiss it without also dismissing something fundamental about oneself.

Have you ever encountered someone who makes the claim of pointless rehashing, who is also the Wicked Witch of the West or a hoarder or a serial monogamist or someone who drinks herself into a coma every night? Isn't living in the grip of such addictive behaviors an indication of fear and anxiety about the past? How can anyone begin to heal from such wounds until they are willing to examine them?

At its basis, ignoring the past is a denial of truth. Anything we are unable or afraid to consider has power over us and drives our behavior in secret but destructive ways. Refusal to attempt *self-knowledge*, as the saints call this introspection, is unhealthy. Without self-knowledge we lack self-discipline and self-control; we destroy ourselves and others. "Those who don't know history are destined to repeat it."[2]

> Whoever wants to remain faithful to his baptismal promises and resist temptations will want to adopt the means for doing so: self-knowledge, practice of an ascesis [self-discipline] adapted to the situations that confront him, obedience to God's commandments, exercise of the moral virtues, and fidelity to prayer. (CCC 2340)

The longer I pursued God, the more intimacy and trust I experienced with him—intimacy and trust that quickly became uncomfortable whenever God challenged my deep-seated distortions about who he is and what he is like, through my patterns.

Through lovely, terrifying experts I learned that because they are powerless and helpless, children view parents as godlike, and their experiences, therefore, totally shape the understanding of God that children form. My distortions and patterns were rooted in parental beliefs and attitudes, coping mechanisms, and other "baggage" I brought forward from childhood and projected onto God and even other people. The system was built for a reason that no longer exists. It was a survival mechanism for a powerless child in an overwhelming family situation. It served a legitimate purpose at that time, but later became a powerful, secret trap.

We built these self-protective systems and therefore have the power to take them down. Without this recognition, nothing will change. With recognition and determination, daily scripture, and most likely some outside assistance, anything is possible. When I perceived my patterns, I was able to view my situations differently, and my behavior changed for the better. The Holy Spirit was unleashed into my life, and my story was reframed.

God's Pop Quizzes

I spent a lot of time and energy in my early twenties pursuing holiness and getting rid of the "biggie" sins in my life. Because I was in church ministry, I felt I had to conquer these glaring faults, such as smoking and drinking; the obsessive perfectionist in me didn't want to be so obviously hypocritical! I started with smoking, which killed two birds with one stone since I always smoked when I drank. Next I quit cursing—a difficult prospect, for I had a filthy mouth, but I knew it was unladylike and ungodly. In all of these pursuits, which took considerable time, God led me step-by-step, sometimes second-by-second, and leaning completely on him, I was able to conquer these areas.

You can imagine my discouragement, then, when God began prompting me about my hidden faults. I began studying the effects of sin, including mistakes and things I felt I couldn't help. My raging temper? *I can't help that*, I would think, as I put holes in several walls and deflated the spirits of other people with my angriness.

By that time, however, God had gripped my soul, and I wanted nothing less than to please him; I was willing to hear that I had to follow Jesus down this narrow road in order to strive for the holiness that would bring me closer to God, and the prospect of being rid of an explosive pain I had carried my whole life became my Promised Land.

That I could help my rage and that I was responsible for changing it was the most daunting prospect, more so as God began to reveal how deeply the roots were buried. As he began teaching me about it, I would experience *pop quizzes*, painful relationships and circumstances that triggered ugly behaviors—all opportunities to examine what God was teaching me that left me drained and exhausted.

The Church calls these pop quizzes "trials, temptations, and tests."

> The Holy Spirit makes us discern between trials, which are necessary for the growth of the inner man, and temptation, which leads to sin and death. We must also discern between being tempted and consenting to temptation. Finally, discernment unmasks the lie of temptation, whose object appears to be good, a "delight to the eyes" and desirable, when in reality its fruit is death. God does not want to impose the good, but wants free beings. . . . There is a certain usefulness to temptation. No one but God knows what our soul has received from him, not even we ourselves. But temptation reveals it in order to teach us to know ourselves, and in this way we discover our evil inclinations [predominant fault] and are obliged to give thanks for the goods that temptation has revealed to us. (CCC 2847–48)

I failed a great many of these pop quizzes until I discerned their pattern and usefulness, and this failure led to bouts of depression as my obsessive perfectionism was triggered. To relieve the feelings of depression, I would self-medicate. God had a better plan. He began the deep excavation: eradicating my predominant fault, the most painful work of my life.

Inward Journey

Everyone has a predominant fault, and it is spoken of in the scriptures as "the sin that clings to us" (Heb 12:1, NAB), a self-imposed variety of "cross." If you are unaware of your

predominant fault, the Church's mystics say it is easiest to
detect early, before it becomes hidden in the guise of righteousness: pride covers in the appearance of generosity and
nobility, while laziness covers in the appearance of humility.

We might ask God for truth and light, if we sincerely do
not know what this fault is. The Lord offers us many opportunities for discernment, especially when we have a steady
diet of scripture. We could also ask our spiritual director, for
he often knows us far better than we know ourselves and
sees where we deceive ourselves. But for me it was really a
very simple exercise: what triggers my very worst emotional
binges? My depressive episodes?

The Lord led me to scriptures, books, pastors, mentors,
and helpers that continually reminded me of the psychology behind depression: Depression is most often caused
by anger. When unexpressed or suppressed, anger goes
underground and becomes depression. Anger is a stress
reaction that stimulates chemical reactions in the body that,
if maintained, cause imbalances. This is why medication
(self-medicated or otherwise) without discernment of the
root cause can abort the natural process of depression, which
is the letting go of something no longer useful.

My most violent emotional reactions were triggered
by the stimulation of childhood coping mechanisms that
were no longer useful or appropriate, and that needed to be
uprooted from my life. "When I was a child, I spoke like a
child, I thought like a child, I reasoned like a child; when I
became a man, I gave up childish ways" (1 Cor 13:11, RSV).

These outgrown coping mechanisms were formed
unconsciously when, as a little girl, I was faced with emotions and circumstances within my family that I was too
young to understand or handle. They were the way my
subconscious protected me, a precious method of self-
preservation, and I thank God for them.

As an adult, however, they continued to operate on an
unconscious level, triggered by what are called "historical

emotions." They were no longer useful or appropriate simply because I had become an adult who was capable of understanding and coping with painful circumstances and emotions. To revert to childhood coping mechanisms is like an adult who relies on a pacifier to solve a problem. Impossible. Silly. The coping mechanism, operating unconsciously, becomes an ingrained impediment to my unleashing.

As Fr. Lagrange said in *The Three Ages of the Interior Life,* the weakest point of our soul, the predominant fault, is where the enemy exploits us most. If left unaddressed, this blockage will lead to comfort seeking, and can ultimately cause us to forfeit the Promised Land. God is profoundly concerned with our predominant fault, because in it lie the clues to what prevents our oneness with him, the supreme desire of his heart and the key to an unleashed life.

My predominant fault is raging rebellion, triggered by feelings of powerlessness and hurt in the hands of authoritative men. You probably have a different one. Perhaps you have a different trigger. For me, men I respected or who were in positions of authority who criticized me triggered explosive binges of rage that could last hours, days, or weeks. Usually it was a minor criticism, but I went over the edge and jumped with both feet into blatant rebellion, usually to show him just how powerful and uncontrollable I could be.

The need for control and to be above criticism led to obsessive perfectionism through which I *seemed* to be in control and able to avoid painful criticism. I was only motivated to excavate this idea when I found myself imposing aggressive authority and obsessive compulsiveness on my children. I was terrified I would do to them what my father's parenting style had done to me. After I learned to control my aggressive rage, an inability to be perfect in any area triggered depression—inward, self-directed rage.

Gently but persistently, the Lord proposed that making excuses for my predominant fault or otherwise denying that I was responsible for it, or believing I was unable to control it, is denial of the truth, and a subtle tactic of the enemy to keep me mired in it. At their very root, rage (aggressive anger) and depression (passive anger) are both a mask for something even deeper, something Jesus probes insistently: pain and fear. Like the woman caught in adultery, my pain is always the signpost pointing to the place Jesus longs to heal me. I am not condemned, but I must leave my sin habit behind.

My pain and fear lie in feelings of worthlessness. My rage, passive and aggressive, was the mask that covered my pain and fear. Is it not true of all of us? Isn't your pain and fear covered by anger that is provoked particularly when your predominant fault is triggered? Can you see how this fault can be an interior enemy, the one that enslaves us, a secret poison and prison? "Everyone who commits sin is a slave to sin" (Jn 8:34).

I must be especially aware of the temptation to laziness that says my predominant fault can never be completely eradicated. If it were not possible, God would not have commanded me to "be holy, for I am holy" (1 Pt 1:16). "You shall love the Lord your God with all your heart, and with all your soul, and with all your strength, and with all your mind; and your neighbor as yourself" (Lk 10:27). This is my calling and opus, that of every man.

Once I discern the predominant fault and begin to combat it, trials and temptations along this line become opportunities to progress and growth. When the predominant fault is conquered, I am free to love God and my neighbor sacrificially and purely, like God loves and lives. I am unleashed.

I am at rest, participating in eternal life here on earth. I have grown into myself plus grace, my supernatural self, minus the defects. My integrated, whole, healed personality can then attract others to Jesus in me. What a hope!

Comfort Seeking

In *The Road Less Traveled,* Dr. Scott Peck observes that the
road to wholeness always involves periods of pain and
difficulty.

> Life is difficult. . . . What makes life difficult is
> that the process of confronting and solving prob-
> lems is a painful one. Problems, depending upon
> their nature, evoke in us frustration or grief or
> sadness or loneliness or guilt or regret or anger
> or fear or anxiety or anguish or despair. These
> are uncomfortable feelings, often very uncom-
> fortable, often as painful as any kind of physical
> pain, sometimes equaling the very worst kind of
> physical pain. Indeed, it is because of the pain
> that events or conflicts engender in us that we call
> them problems. And since life poses an endless
> series of problems, life is always difficult and is
> full of pain as well as joy.[3]

As I walked with God and found my wounds probed
ever more deeply with his persistent finger, at times I was
tempted to turn away from him in order to seek external
comforts. God knows we are children. He knows we need
comfort. He knows our pains make us seek places of refuge,
relief, and safety. He longs to be our comfort, our refuge and
strength, our lover, our provider, the one who is not only
able to touch us more deeply, deliberately, and thoroughly
than any mortal, but is ever present and ever willing to do
so in every trouble. But he cannot provide comfort for us
when we are busy seeking and grasping it for ourselves.

Ultimately, comfort seeking is a denial of the need to
change. We may seek comfort in relationships, drugs or
alcohol, food, shopping, pornography, work. But comfort
seeking can only give fleeting relief, and what's worse is that
we may just discover we have become mired in destructive,

addictive behaviors and habits we feel unable to control. We may even wake up to find that, although we may desire to inherit the promise of freedom, we are in bondage and addicted, and the Promised Land is no longer attractive, even though it is still on the horizon.

As I reached for outward comforts, the Holy Spirit invited me to think of addictions and other destructive behaviors as attempts at external comfort seeking and self-medication; they are an outward grasping for love. What might I be forfeiting by my outward reaching? The love God longed to unleash into my lonely soul. The Holy Spirit was attracted to my pain and need, but I was numb rather than receiving him there.

Hebrews 12 instructs us that it is in those times when we get discouraged and faint that we most need to consider Jesus.

> Therefore, since we are surrounded by so great a cloud of witnesses [saints and angels who help us], let us also lay aside [strip off] every weight, and sin [weakness, fault, and sin] which clings so closely, and let us run with perseverance the race that is set before us, looking to Jesus the pioneer [the first] and perfecter [and last] of our faith, who for the sake of the joy that was set before him endured the cross, despising the shame, and is seated at the right hand of the throne of God. Consider him who endured from sinners such hostility against himself, so that you may not grow weary or fainthearted. In your struggle against sin you have not yet resisted to the point of shedding your blood. (Heb 12:1–4)

Talk about unleashed! According to verses 3–11, the purpose of this whole passage is to instruct in the reason for difficulties and temptations. Rather than punishment or revenge, these verses remind us that trials are discipline and teaching in the way of holiness for those who are willingly "trained" by them.

In Hebrews 12:1, this way of holiness is said to be a kind of marathon. We are even told what specific areas of our marathons, our lives, are being corrected through trials: "Therefore lift your *drooping* hands and strengthen your *weak* knees, and make straight paths for your feet, so that what is *lame* may not be put *out of joint* but rather be healed" (Heb 12:12–13, emphasis added). Every *iniquity* (what is crooked or not straight, meaning sin), every area that is *weak* and *lame* and *broken,* must be healed.

There is also a warning against comfort seeking. "See to it that . . . no one be immoral or irreligious like Esau, who sold his birthright for a single meal. For you know that afterward, when he desired to inherit the blessing, he was rejected, for he found no chance to repent, though he sought it with tears" (Heb 12:15–17).

The Old Testament account of Esau's comfort seeking is related in a few short sentences.

> Once when Jacob was boiling pottage, Esau came in from the field, and he was famished. And Esau said to Jacob, "Let me eat some of that red pottage, for I am famished!" . . . Jacob said, "First sell me your birthright." Esau said, "I am about to die; of what use is a birthright to me?" Jacob said, "Swear to me first." So he swore to him, and sold his birthright to Jacob. Then Jacob gave Esau bread and pottage of lentils, and he ate and drank, and rose and went his way. Thus Esau despised his birthright. (Gn 25:29–34)

The birthright in that time was a great honor. Because he would succeed the father and shepherd of the tribe in responsibility, the firstborn was entitled to a double-portion inheritance and to his father's particular blessing. The birthright embraced the responsibility and rule of family and

tribe, and most importantly the "blessing of the promise" of
Abraham, which included the future possession of Canaan
and covenant relationship with God. The blessings Esau
was entitled to were both material and spiritual, as they are
for us. Jesus, as the firstborn of all creation, inherited this
blessing, and we inherit it with him (Col 1:12–18).

With the words, "I am about to die; of what use is a
birthright to me?" Esau revealed that the death of his flesh
(which was simply a strong hunger) was more important
than the death of his spirit, that the birthright was worthless
and held no value for him in the face of his lust for comfort.

Jacob was boiling lentil stew, and Esau came in from
the "field" and was "faint" and wanted some of Jacob's food.
This account serves as a warning for us. Spiritually speaking, when we have been long in the field of the soul, are
we not naturally in need of nourishment, physical or otherwise? Any long presence in the field may leave us needy.
But a simple, normal need for food led Esau to the perverted
presumption that he could get back his spiritual inheritance
once his belly was full.

That was not the case, however. We see in Hebrews
that Esau's presumption led him to forfeit his inheritance,
even though he showed a superficial sorrow for the consequences, because there was no true repentance in it. What
we know about Esau from this story is that his heart was
not with God, as his actions proved. The consequences of
my comfort seeking could often be far more extensive than I
dared to consider while I was busily satisfying my need for
satiation. How much time have I wasted in addiction and
destructive habits that I can never get back? Whom have I
hurt in the process of comfort seeking? What relationships
have I damaged?

This is exactly the danger of comfort seeking God
warned me about in my walk with him. My inheritance is
him (Gn 15:1). What a grave and dangerous presumption to
believe God will allow me to ignore the call to healing and

salvation (my inheritance) without a single consequence. How long can I deny the truth he attempts repeatedly to tell and show me through circumstances and negative emotions, or to artificially seek comfort from anything, especially those things that could ultimately enslave me and keep me from him?

The Bible is full of God's promises of provision and consolation. St. John of the Cross, especially, teaches we must wait for God. I must persevere under the pain long enough for it to do its work of instruction and purification. I must trust him. I am a witness that there is truly purpose behind every trial we experience and suffer. God is moving on, in, and through us. We are being unleashed. I was invited to believe and trust that trials are not arbitrary or God's attempt to get even with me for sin. He has no need of that, for sin has its own inherent consequences, and they are designed to teach me to choose more wisely.

He is humility and meekness. I can trust this matchless power. "Come to me, all who labor and are heavy laden, and I will give you rest. Take my yoke upon you, and learn from me; for I am gentle and lowly in heart, and you will find rest for your souls. For my yoke is easy, and my burden is light" (Mt 11:28–30). The Church has always taught that if for one second of our lives he ceased to love us, we would cease to exist. We are safe with him. He does not condemn or berate; he beckons.

Like the woman caught in adultery, unhealed wounds, sin, and faults lead me to comfort seeking that will, if I continue in it, cause me to permanently forfeit my inheritance simply because I am unable any longer to desire it. Presumption tells me there is no need to work so hard and that it will be there later when I want it. But the scriptures teach that this is a grave lie, "immoral and profane" (Heb 12:16, NAB).

The mystics maintain that the work of healing is the most important work of life; it is sanctification; it is salvation; it is unleashed *life*. "How shall we escape if we neglect

such a great salvation?" (Heb 2:3). To neglect this work is to
stunt my capacity to receive God, and whatever stage and
capacity I allow him to achieve in me here is the stage and
capacity with which I enter heaven (Eccl 11:3).

This has always been the teaching of the Church. St.
Augustine said, "He who shall not have cultivated his field
(the soul) shall after this life experience [either] the fire of
purgation or eternal punishment" (see also 1 Cor 3:15).[4]
"When evening comes, you will be examined in love," said
St. John of the Cross.[5]

Jesus is very clear throughout the scriptures that only
those who continue to follow and persevere to the end
receive the full inheritance. Jesus did not seek comfort, yet
he always received it at the proper time from God's hand
(Mt 4:11; 17:1–7). "Jesus said to him, 'No one who puts his
hand to the plow and looks back is fit for the kingdom of
God'" (Lk 9:62). The kingdom of God is our inheritance
with Christ.

Jesus was worthy, for he "endured the cross, despising
its shame." God teaches all his sons and daughters this way
(Heb 12:2–10). The letter to the Hebrews teaches us to look
to him, and like him, to keep our eyes on the inheritance,
the joy set before us. The joy set before Jesus was wonderful
enough to help him endure humiliation, torture, beatings,
mockery, being spit on, and crucifixion. That must be some
unspeakably superabundant inheritance!

When God began to unleash me, I experienced painful,
negative feelings, but through various means, especially
the scriptures, he always assured me that they are part of a
normal process of giving up the old ways of knowing and
doing. They are a necessary part of salvation and learning
to hear God. In times of depression and violent negative
emotion, when self-knowledge becomes painful, when experiencing the pain of offenses and circumstances in an effort
to hear God speak through them, please do not seek external
comfort. Wait on God. Wait, my friend, for he always comes,

and he will whisper the glories of your salvation to you and renew your strength. You will mount up with wings of eagles, you will run and not tire, you shall walk with him and not faint (Is 40:31), and you will find God unleashed in ways you never dreamed.

Let's Review

Let's review how God unleashes us from our destructive patterns of behavior:

> *The Holy Spirit attempts to alert me* through various provocations that my behavior is destructive, and therefore sinful.
>
> *These provocations will become more and more disruptive and painful* as I fail to hear him.
>
> *I can discern my predominant fault, the deepest place* where God wants to unleash me, through my sin patterns.
>
> *I live an unleashed life to the extent that I embrace virtue,* leaving behind my former ways and patterns of behavior.
>
> *The Holy Spirit works in my outward habits and behaviors first,* then moves to interior motives and errors in perceptions.
>
> *I must guard against the temptation to seek outside comfort* as he probes and heals the wounds that trigger my predominant fault, because comfort seeking is a trap that can keep me mired in sin. If I only ask and wait, he will give me the grace to cling to the promise that he will comfort me.

An Invitation

Dear One, I am holding your hand. I have prayed for you with great fervor, because I *know* what you might feel. As

you sit with God right now, I pray you will dare to examine
your worst behaviors. You may not be able to completely
answer every question yet, but if you truly open your interior home to him, I believe the Holy Spirit will whisper
through and quicken your heart, especially as you continue
through the coming chapters and probe your circumstances,
relationships, and desires.

You may want to begin keeping track of your progress
in a prayer journal. The regular, systematic reading of scripture—whether you follow along in the daily readings or sys-
tematically work your way through a book of the Bible, such
as the psalms or the gospels—is an essential part of learning
to hear God's voice. It is also the best way to learn to identify
your predominant fault and to recognize the patterns God is
using in your life to draw your attention to what is most in
need of healing. As you read, ask yourself: What is the Holy
Spirit saying to you through these verses? Write it down,
and over time you will begin to see the patterns emerge.

For example, the first principle God taught me about
my explosive anger was in Psalm 4:4–5. The first time I read
this passage, I was drawn to just the first few words. Each
time I meditated on this passage, my heart rested on a different place as God spoke to me directly through his Word.

"*Be angry, but sin not*; commune [meditate] with your
own hearts on your beds, and be silent. Offer right sacrifices,
and put your trust in the LORD." I felt the Lord impressing on
me that when I got angry, even explosively angry, he wanted
me to control my behavior—no shouting or violence.

"Be angry, but sin not; *commune with your own hearts on
your beds, and be silent.* Offer right sacrifices, and put your
trust in the Lord." This part let me know he wanted me to
talk to him about it, *all* of it, the whole truth, privately in the
silence of my heart and/or in my prayer journal.

"Be angry, but sin not; commune with your own hearts
on your beds, and be silent. *Offer right sacrifices,* and put your
trust in the LORD." With this, he led me to understand that

if I needed to take action in some way, we would decide together. Maybe I needed to speak out, gently and with love and truth, on my own or on another's behalf. Usually, I just needed to let the "offense" pass in charity.

As I learned proper boundaries, there were times I had to outwardly "offer right sacrifices" (which just means do the right thing), but I learned to never react out of emotion, impulse, or provocation. I don't always succeed, but I am never condemned when I am sincerely and consistently trying my best.

"Be angry, but sin not; commune with your own hearts on your beds, and be silent. Offer right sacrifices, and *put your trust in the LORD*." While I waited in silence, I was to trust him with the consequences and ultimate outcome of my outpouring to him. Often when my anger was provoked, I would beg him to defend me. Sometimes he did, in secret ways and without my input. But most often, I learned I was hypersensitive and easily offended and simply needed to forgive and overlook the "offense." I needed to grow in charity.

Is God speaking to you through this verse? What is he saying? If this passage doesn't resonate with you, continue reading and listening as the Word is proclaimed at Mass, until you sense God is speaking to you. If you are unsure, talk to a priest or spiritual director, who can help you to discern.

As you read, you may experience deep pain; do your best to express all of it to God.

God Prompt

Deep wounds and pain make us rebellious and angry, provoking aggressive, sinful, comfort-seeking behaviors. Such sinful behaviors destroy relationships. In my case, my marriage suffered; my parenting degenerated; I developed self-medicating habits. The death and destruction in the wake of my anger pointed out the sin of it. God specifically allowed repeated provocation of my most painful, negative feelings; he purposely allowed the infliction of my greatest pains in order to point out my faults and invite me to work with him to begin rooting out my faults and sin patterns.

This is the process I still go through when I find myself tempted to practice or actually practicing my predominant fault and other destructive behavior patterns. For me there were many memories that had to be exposed and confronted. I can always trace my worst temptations back to this root. Once I recognize it as "my Daddy thing," it ceases to have power over me, and I am able, instead, to practice virtue. That is the point at which I realize I have been unleashed.

Dear One, your behavior patterns also reveal your predominant fault. Your predominant fault is where God is unleashing you, and is already at work. He wants you to join him.

Attempt to discern the predominant fault: Do your best to name your worst behavior pattern or habit. See if you can identify the prevailing sin behind your behavior pattern: lust, gluttony, greed, jealousy, rebellion, anger, fear? How often would you say acting on your habit or habits could be narrowed down to this prevailing sin?

Probe for the root: As you spend some time evaluating the history of your life in God's presence, is your worst behavior pattern triggered by a particular emotion? Talk to God about all the circumstances, and pour out all your feelings of this memory.

Gathering and articulating may take considerable time, but please do not rush. Try very hard not to numb the pain; the memories must be completely felt to be completely healed. As you are able to do so, privately talk with the Lord about what you are discovering, and trust him to guide you to heal your soul and unleash you from inflicting any more pain, especially on those you love. Do not hold anything back from the Great Physician, who longs to heal you completely. If you persevere with him, you will one day be free of those habits that prevent you from experiencing an unleashed life. I am living proof.

Be ready for God's pop quizzes in your life! If you undertake this kind of spiritual exercise with any sincerity or depth, you will probably be offered a pop quiz—a surprise temptation or test—in the very near future. Please consider it a loving and fortuitous opportunity from the Holy Spirit to practice what he is teaching, and *not* a punishment. I hope you will pray now for eyes to see and ears to hear it for what it is when it comes. You may fail repeatedly in the short term, until you become accustomed to recognizing your predominant fault, its root, and how it controls your behavior. I pray you will cling to the assurance of your Promised Land, and the knowledge that you are surely progressing through the upward spiral. The process is necessarily slow and painful, but I can promise it gets better and easier with perseverance. I have prayed for you with great empathy. I believe you're going to see incredible things happen in your life as you practice! Praise God, "who alone does *wondrous* things" (Ps 72:18, emphasis added).

Otherwise, pray for yourself and all the people in your life that you know need an unleashing from God:

> Come Holy Spirit, fill the hearts of your faithful and kindle in them the fire of your love. Send forth your Spirit and they shall be created. And you shall renew the face of the earth. O, God, who by the light of the Holy Spirit, did instruct the hearts of the faithful, grant that by the same Holy Spirit we may be truly wise and ever enjoy his consolations, through Christ, our Lord. Amen.

4

*W*hy Do You See the Speck in Your Neighbor's Eye, but Do Not Notice the Log in Your Own Eye?

Matthew 7:3

Surrendering Judgment to Peace

I wonder how it felt, sitting on the grass with the wildflowers nodding in the breeze, watching the ripples glinting on the lake in the distance, the human race hearing such radical things for the first time.

"Go the extra mile. . . . Love your enemy. . . . Don't worry. . . . Stockpile treasure . . . in *heaven*. . . . Blessed are the poor, the depressed, those who let others go first, the hungry and thirsty, the martyred and persecuted. Adultery is also a matter of the heart. We are judged in the measure we ourselves judge."

What would it have been like, to be part of that crowd? Did the grass sing? Did the earth pound with the new truths, the new order he unleashed with every word?

"Why do you see the speck . . . ?"

Jesus' question, here, concerns all our relationships. Whether superficial or intimate, with family or acquaintances, relating well to others can be sticky business—maybe the stickiest, since the beautiful messiness of love is often involved. We all know what it's like to walk on eggshells as we navigate the painful and difficult parts of such relationships, perhaps especially with people we truly love.

The morning after every Thanksgiving I laugh at the number of news and talk-show commentators who make halfhearted jokes about the awfulness of their Thanksgiving holiday gathering, where everyone of different stripes is thrown together for hours of "giving thanks."

Someone got drunk, someone restarted a long-standing feud, someone else had nothing nice to say about another's kids, someone whined about being the less-favored black sheep of the family. Someone seems to think he knows everything about everything there is to know, bragged until someone else gagged, or pointed out someone's weight gain . . . and on and on. Sheesh. At such times close or frequent contact with family feels impossible. Discerning another's inability to relate in mature and healthy ways due to insecurities and weaknesses seems so obvious to us. When we get a glimpse of another's neediness, it's revolting and irritating. Why is that?

Let's not leave out work and church families. Aren't there personalities at your workplace or church that you simply cannot abide? Those who gossip or are passive-aggressive? The ones who refuse to get involved but attack and complain when others do? Maybe it's that coworker who repeatedly overcommits, then fails to follow through? Or, alternately, the one who tries to control and overplan and overanalyze, creating little fiefdoms that disallow others to contribute? With each encounter, don't you sometimes feel you'd rather just be alone?

Receiving Truth in Relationships

Problems—behavioral, relational, and circumstantial—are an invitation to self-knowledge. And because self-knowledge leads directly to humility, and therefore love, the mystics assert it is the foundation necessary for progress in the spiritual life. And so we need other people, because relationships—especially the repeats and problems associated with these human interactions—can assist in our spiritual growth and unleashing.

When my oldest son was three or four, he liked to dress himself. One afternoon when we were late and headed out the door, I noticed he had on one bright green sock and one red one. I had to stifle the urge to make him change his socks before we left the house. If the Holy Spirit and both our guardian angels had not been defending the door of my mouth (because I had begun asking them to), I know I would have demanded my little boy change his socks and thereby undermined his confidence in his ability to dress himself.

Instead the Holy Spirit nudged my spirit, *What will it hurt to allow him to wear mismatched socks?* I remember thinking, *Not a single thing but my ugly pride.*

Unleashed!

Isn't this knowing also relationship? As we know and love ourselves more purely, we can know and love God and others more purely. The essence of the two greatest commands to love God and love our neighbor—growing in holiness—is growth in relationships.

What might it mean for us, then, that God exists in relationship? Well first, if the Trinity is the mature, fruitful relationship between the persons of God—all distinct, all one, all operating with a single will and single heart, as the Church has always taught—can we entertain the fantasy that we can grow, spiritually, apart from our relationships?

When I have been obsessively needy or dependent on others, God repeatedly prompted me to ask and depend solely on him for my needs. Conversely, when I learned to depend on him and then wanted to go live apart from difficult relationships, God nudged me back toward relationships, cultivating the idea that it is through others that he provides for my growth; difficulties in relating indicate places in which God wants to work in me. Either way, my communion with him and my communion with his family grows.

Because God draws me into the interrelated balance of the Trinity, he unleashes me *and* those around me at the same time. He allows us to work on each other, sometimes like sandpaper. My relationships are always teaching me, but no matter how he speaks through the people around me, the focus is always on me, not them.

This is one way to discern when God is trying to teach us something in our relationships: *When God is speaking to me, he is speaking about me.* Focusing on myself when he speaks (self-knowledge) draws me to what I don't like about myself. We need our difficult relationship challenges and conflicts to point out how and where God wants to unleash us.

Truth through Relationships?

The essence of the Trinity is a total self-giving among the three Persons that unleashes abundant *life*. In most cases, my relationships—perhaps particularly the most difficult ones—are deliberately and specifically allowed by the Holy Spirit to draw me to a total, mature, healthy self-giving that unleashes abundant life for me and the other.

All our relationships and contacts can teach us things. So what does it mean when certain encounters or certain kinds of people provoke intense emotional eruptions in us? If we want to grow in the spiritual life, we need to take a closer look at our reactions, and consider the possibility that, far from conflict simply being the (probably oblivious) other persons' fault, God may be using these relationships to unleash us. For this reason the very people we might consider some sort of enemy are our spiritual allies.

In Genesis 4 we find a dramatic example. We are presented with very different personalities in two of Adam and Eve's sons. Cain is the hunter-gatherer, the aggressive conqueror. Abel is more laid-back, a farmer, probably far more patient than his brother. Crops don't grow quickly, after all.

Their differences lead them to make different offerings to God, offerings that illustrate something about their spiritual conditions. God's preference for Abel's sacrifice and disregard for Cain's provokes an intense reaction within Cain. He has an eruption. He is depressed. "His countenance has fallen." But that is only the surface. Like the enormous, hidden underbelly of a seemingly small iceberg, what lies beneath his depression is rage.

God and Cain have an exchange about this eruption of emotion in Cain: "The Lord said to Cain, 'Why are you angry, and why has your countenance fallen? If you do well, will you not be accepted? And if you do not do well, sin is couching at the door; its desire is for you, but you must master it'" (Gn 4:6–7). So many times God used this passage of scripture as an invitation for me to confront my rage, a rage that destroys all who live with me when it is in action. Why am I angry? If I do well and call on God, will I not be forgiven? If I neglect to deal with my anger toward others, sin will devour me and those around me. But I can master it through the grace and love of Christ.

Characteristic of the scriptures, it is supremely understated, but we know that Cain experienced an emotional binge through his behavior toward his brother. We know he did not do well in his relationship. We know he did not call on God for help. He succumbed to the crouching rage and murdered his brother.

God's response to Cain's emotion tells us we are responsible for the behaviors provoked by our own emotions in our relationships. The Lord is there to help us through our eruptions, but we should learn to ask for his help, his forgiveness, his correction, and his direction *before* we spew our destruction on every living thing within a mile radius. Otherwise, the cycle continues unbroken and we remain in its grip. How does God offer us repeated opportunities to ask him for help? What if he offers us "relationship repeats"?

My Relationship Patterns Tell the Truth

We date, work for, work with, make friends with, and marry the kinds of people who wounded us earliest and deepest. The longer we go without addressing our relationship patterns, the longer we repeat patterns of bad relationships and continue unhealthy boundaries in them.

As adults, the people we choose to allow into our lives can trigger negative emotions and even emotional eruptions that call forth deep-seated pain and wounds. These are places that are bound up in anger and pain, places in which the Holy Spirit wants to unleash us. God can use the negative emotions to change us. The themes that are predominate in our relationships—anger, people pleasing, control, immaturity, noncommitment, pretension, dishonesty, cheating—also dominate our memories. To some degree, this is true for all of us. The past shapes our visions, which in turn defines who and what we see, and who and what we seek.

One of a multitude in the scriptures, Cain and Abel's family portrait reveals the way God allows relationships as a tool for self-knowledge. In the first epistle of John, we learn the reason Cain killed Abel: ". . . we should love one another, and not be like Cain who was of the evil one and murdered his brother. And why did he murder him? Because his own deeds were evil and his brother's righteous" (1 Jn 3:11–12). There was something sinful under the surface of Cain's emotions, something that, left unchecked and unhealed, would be deadly. How foreboding.

Abel's acceptable sacrifice triggered an eruption in Cain which should have sent him to God to sort out his hurt, motivations, emotions, and desires. God took the initiative and extended truth, and the opportunity for forgiveness and healing, but Cain did not avail himself of it. The murder he cherished in his heart came forth from his hand.

Afterward, Cain became paranoid, projecting his own murderous spirit onto nameless others. He worried he would be murdered by another. We are always projecting on others the thing we are. Is this not why God allowed Cain to be jealous of and provoked by Abel: to reveal his murderous rage to him in the hope he would go to God with it and seek healing?

Over and over, because my predominant fault is anger and rebellion, my boyfriends, ex-fiancé, husband, pastors, and employers were all similar personality types; they all triggered the same type of emotional eruption within me. I was attracted to that type of personality, until the inevitable eruption. My eruptions revealed buried emotion and wounds, but I was very slow in discerning the pattern. At some point I just got so sick of repeating the same type of relationships, I finally asked him, "Why am I doing this?" Faithfully, the Holy Spirit was showing me where he wanted to work all along. The pattern of my relationships revealed where God wanted to work in my predominant fault.

Marriage Unleashed

Because my childhood left me with a hypersensitivity to criticism from men I loved and respected, I found myself repeating this pattern as an adult. By the grace of God I let go of a disrespectful relationship with a critical fiancé, who also had certain moral faults I could not tolerate. I knew the man I eventually married loved me dearly, and yet several years into marriage, I discovered that the inevitable criticisms from my husband were also extremely painful. I began acting out, sometimes in rage, as had been my practice for years.

As a non-Catholic, all I knew about marriage was that it was primarily a *vow*. I was promising God all the things I spoke to my husband. That knowledge forced me to stay when I wanted to leave. My respect for a vow forced me to deal with my emotions and the ways I was acting out when I didn't want to.

I didn't know at the time that God speaks to our world about himself through marital union. "God disposed man and woman for each other so that they might be 'no longer two, but one'" (Mt 19:6). In this way they are to live in love, be fruitful, and thus become a sign of God himself, who is nothing but overflowing love" (CCC 1601–1605). This is an "outward" purpose of the relationship of marriage, according to the *Catechism of the Catholic Church*. But there's an inward purpose too.

According to the Church, the sacramental grace of matrimony matures the natural love of husband and wife. Because it's sacramental, marital love originates from the Trinity and Christ's love for the Church (Eph 5:22); the grace of the sacrament of Matrimony elevates the natural spousal love to one that's supernatural. This elevation of natural love between spouses far surpasses emotional or physical compatibility. Sacramental grace gives marital love a sanctifying quality, making it an instrument for growth in holiness, and marriage a path to sainthood. My spouse can lead me to heaven and sainthood. Could conflicts in my marriage, then, be an invitation to greater unleashing through my spouse?

Marriage often provokes emotional eruptions that point out an important matter: what is necessary to the health of my marriage is often identical to what is necessary for my personal growth; each of us holds the pieces that the other is missing. If I am dishonest, for example, I might discover that my dishonesty provokes a memory in my spouse that needs to be healed. I will know I have provoked something important in him, not by what he says, but by his emotional "eruption." What are his emotions saying?

Simultaneously, when I am dishonest, I find that I, too, have memories at the hands of others that provoke me to dishonesty, memories that shaped me and need to be healed. I see that my spouse's observations and criticisms of my dishonesty, although painful, are helpful and even necessary for my growth.

In Eruptions, the Message Is in the Memory

Isn't this model true of every relationship that provokes negative emotion, especially eruptions, in relationships we repeat? Sometimes, the relationship will not be as close as a marriage, but it still can be potent in the hands of the Holy Spirit, especially if the emotion (eruption) is repeated.

Memories serve our unleashing, but they are servants who live banished in the dungeon or way up in the attic. Most of the time we forget they're even in the house. But we can't work with them until we let them in the room with us. Working with a memory and the emotion attached to it is not the same as indulging it and letting it run wild throughout the interior castle.

According to psychiatrists, the reason some relationships provoke eruptions in us is because certain kinds of people trigger specific memories—historical emotions—from the past. Our memories aren't pure, and they aren't accurate. But they are important. Their purpose is not historical but spiritual.

We remember events the way we need or want to remember them, because they reveal what was, and continues to be, most important to us. Subconsciously, we pick and choose the specifics; we attach feelings and memories to the wounds we received and remember. Our memories speak volumes about who *we* are, not because they recount completely accurately what has happened to us, but because the Holy Spirit wants to unleash us through them.

We are attracted to certain types of people because we have soul work to do regarding what they provoke in us. This is always true of a marriage partner, children, and immediate family. But not just in marriage and family. Isn't the Holy Spirit working in and through all our relationships? Doesn't every relationship have a message for us? Aren't we all sometimes Cain and sometimes Abel?

For several years after I married, my relationship with my sister was strained and difficult. We grew painfully distant. Although four years my junior, she married soon after I did, and I felt she had a superior attitude about her family that she displayed in subtle but critical ways. We had very different lifestyles and parenting techniques, and I saw her as disparaging my choices. Our relationship became so contentious and snarky that I went to God about it. What was her problem, anyway? This was my reading for the day:

> Why do you see the speck in your neighbor's eye,
> but do not notice the log in your own eye? Or how
> can you say to your neighbor, "Friend, let me take

out the speck in your eye," when you yourself do
not see the log in your own eye? You hypocrite,
first take the log out of your own eye, and then
you will see clearly to take the speck out of your
[neighbor's] eye. (Lk 6:41–42)

Remember I said when God speaks *to* us, he is speaking
about us? I briefly applied this passage to my sister and wal-
lowed in what I thought was God speaking to me about her
hypocrisy. But the Holy Spirit seemed to keep poking his
divine finger into my own heart; I reluctantly examined my
own attitude toward my sister.

I discovered I was the one with the haughty opinion.
It was hard to swallow, but I admitted before the Lord in
prayer that it was true. I was the one with "the problem,"
and I felt terrible that she sensed my self-righteousness. I
took concrete steps to watch my tone of voice and my body
language and to choose supportive, encouraging words
toward her, and guess what? Our relationship improved
immediately. It was me all along.

Jesus has something revealing to say about the people
who trigger our negative emotions. They are our mirrors.
God shows us ourselves through these people, especially the
parts of ourselves that are unacceptable to us, the parts we
repress and deny a voice. They are our teachers. Whatever
offensive faults we see in them are the arrows pointing to
our own hidden faults, often multiplied several times over,
as a log is to a speck.

Often our family members are the ones who both
instill and later provoke negative emotions and sometimes
eruptions in us, but the responsibility is always our own.
We are adults. "Every act directly willed is imputable to its
author: Thus the Lord asked Eve after the sin in the garden:
'What is this that you have done?' He asked Cain the same
question" (CCC 1736). Beyond the natural family, Baptism
incorporates us into God's family, the Church, so it is also

important that our relationships with people we meet there are evaluated.

God Works through His Family

As Jesus pointed out, we tend to draw attention to the faults of others in order to cover our own, but in doing so we disown a shadowy part of ourselves that we find painful or unattractive. St. Paul sheds some light on this subject in his discourse on the Body of Christ, of which each of us is part:

> God arranged the organs in the body, each one of them, as he chose. If all were a single organ, where would the body be? As it is, there are many parts, yet one body. The eye cannot say to the hand, "I have no need of you," nor again the head to the feet, "I have no need of you." On the contrary, the parts of the body which seem to be weaker are indispensable. . . . Now you are the body of Christ and individually members of it. (1 Cor 12:18–22, 27)

My attitude toward my sister told her I had no need of her, but most of our differences were simply variations in our personalities and temperaments. And isn't it the Holy Spirit who gives talents, temperaments, personalities, gifts, and strengths? How can we say we have no need of others' differences?

We truly need one another because although we all have strengths, our strengths often get way out of balance, and we are all necessarily weak in the opposite. I am deliberate and organized, but my strength out of balance produces weakness: obsessive-compulsive disorder, perfectionism, and a tendency to control. I am strong in teaching and speaking gifts but weak in hospitality.

However, being weak in an area does not excuse me from the biblical command to practice virtue as the opportunities arise. I need those who are strong in faith to teach me through their lives how to be unleashed from the illusion of control; I need those who are strong in hospitality to teach me through their hospitality how to give whatever I have and welcome the other.

According to St. Paul our typical attitude toward weaknesses, both in ourselves and others, is to disparage them. Not only do we do this in ourselves individually, but we do it to one another in the Church. Priests, monks, nuns, those who sing beautifully, teach strikingly, or have other visible roles in the Church, are most honored, while those who are invisible seem less honorable. Put another way, those who complain and seem to cause trouble consistently are unpresentable and therefore useless to us, while those who are easiest to get along with are sought out for their talents instead. St. Paul says in 1 Corinthians 12:25 that God uses the whole family of God to draw unity out of disunity. He is bringing our weaknesses and faults into balance.

My tendency to marginalize those I don't like or who provoke negative emotions in me is wrong. When people are in pain, those around them suffer too (1 Cor 12:26). Isn't this true in every area of our lives? When we are in pain, what do we do to those around us, both in our families and in our churches?

After St. Paul shows us the necessity of every member, he says charity (treating others better than they deserve when it is in their best interest) is better than our strengths and gifts (1 Cor 12:31–13:8). People and their issues can provoke our deepest resentments, most violent emotions, ingrained coping mechanisms, and other spiritual trash that must be acknowledged, excavated, and removed if we are ever to be unleashed.

By rejecting the trigger person or running from him or her, we reject or run from a part of ourselves that Jesus wants to unleash. Whether we judge or forgive, the measure of judgment or forgiveness we offer him or her will be the measure we receive ourselves (Lk 6:37–38). Seen in this light, those who seem to be our greatest enemies are actually a source of rich blessing. They are opportunities for humility and love, opportunities for more of God, opportunities to be unleashed.

God Operates through Our Neighbor

Even our "unpresentable" neighbor is far more important to our own spiritual growth than we first assume. St. Catherine of Siena put it so beautifully:

> I would have you know that every virtue of yours and every defect is put into action by means of your neighbor—every evil. For, if [one] does not love Me, she cannot be in charity with her neighbor; and thus, all evils derive from the soul's deprivation of love of Me and her neighbor. The same is true of many of my gifts and graces, virtues and other spiritual gifts, and those things necessary for the body and human life. I have distributed them all in such a way that no one has all of them. Thus I have given you reason—necessity, in fact—to practice mutual charity. For I could well have supplied each of you with all your needs, both spiritual and material. But I wanted to make you dependent on one another so that each of you could be my minister, dispensing the graces and gifts you have received from me. . . . So you see, I have made you my ministers, setting you in different positions and in different ranks to exercise the virtue of charity.[1]

According to Jesus, our neighbor is everyone.

Loving Aunt Betty

The only word that adequately described Aunt Betty was *crusty*, and I will never forget what an implausible but profound teacher she was—the unlikely deliverer of one of the most mysterious admonitions of my life. She was a child of the twenties, my husband's great aunt, and his grandmother's sister-in-law and best cohort.

Family tradition says Aunt Betty and Nancy got into all kinds of impropriety as young women—that is, until, in Aunt Betty's words, Nancy "got religion" and quit wearing shorts and smoking. Black and whites show the two of them standing by classic cars in vintage swimsuits with cigarettes dangling from glamorous fingers, always gorgeous painted ladies with a glint of trouble in their eyes.

The two prevailing rumors about Aunt Betty, twice a widow, were that she had gotten a little too wild in her heyday and was never able to have children, and that she was rich beyond imagination after outliving the Great Depression and two husbands. She would harangue you in a heartbeat with an infantryman's vocabulary, her voice deep and grainy from decades of smoking. When her health declined and there was no husband or child to help care for her during the day, I would reluctantly make a day trip every month or so with my four-year-old son to clean her hermitage, shop for her, and take her to the doctor when needed.

Because she was so cynical, I never allowed her to pay me, and looking back, I am so thankful I had at least that bit of real charity. I dreaded those trips, mostly because she had some of the coarsest manners I had ever witnessed in a female, young or old. I was always afraid she would say something hurtful or scandalous within earshot of my young son.

The air in her tiny house was cloying with cigarette smoke almost thick enough to lean against. After spending any amount of time there, I felt I might need to be fumigated and radiated for cancer upon departure. The stale smoke hung in my hair and clothes on the trip home, making any other endeavor of the day pretty unpleasant before I had a bath.

Aunt Betty lived almost an hour away, and we were barely able to afford the gas, but there was no one else in the family with the time during the day to help her, so I felt I was doing my "Christian duty" on those once-a-month trips. I knew I was pleasing God by helping her, and if I desired anything, it was to please him.

I was not Catholic at that time, and my church was undergoing a horrible split. Everyone had taken a side, and having been on the wrong side of another split in the same church years before, I knew how evil the insurrection against our pastor was, because God had carefully corrected me for the same thing and taught me significantly about rebellion. The conspirators were in blatant sin, and it bothered me that God did nothing about it. I wanted him to throw thunderbolts from heaven and incinerate them with his word.

With this hypocritical conflict broiling in my heart, I was at the foot of Aunt Betty's toilet, brutally scrubbing weeks-old feces out of her pink shag carpet. Fiercely independent and self-sufficient, she clung vehemently to remaining in her home as long as possible, but it became increasingly difficult for her to get around, and she routinely had accidents while trying to make it to the restroom.

I know she detested that it was necessary for anyone to have to perform such a task for her. Everyone despises his own neediness and the weakness of others. It seems so pathetic. We avert our eyes and awareness in embarrassment and detest acknowledging it, unless it's to criticize. Characteristic of her generation, she never asked me to clean her carpet, and to save her the embarrassment of her "weakness" and "neediness" I never mentioned when I did.

Instead, I fumed at the presumption and pride of those gossiping backbiters who were ripping apart God's beloved church, and the angry action of scrubbing her carpet became something of a soothing metaphor.

As I struggled, God laid a silent question on the altar of my heart, a subtle challenge: why was I on my knees, sweating and scouring the foul carpet in front of me? Shocked, I did not have a ready answer, so I scrubbed and wondered. Why *was* I struggling with that dirty task for a woman to whom I was only remotely related?

While the television in the next room blared with court shows, the answer rolled over me the way my son drove Hot Wheels up and down Aunt Betty's legs. In waves of penetrating astonishment I realized I was willing to clean excrement out of her carpet without any kind of acknowledgment of what I had done because I loved the crusty old woman. She rarely had a nice thing to say, yet I had fallen in love with her because in her weakness she needed me.

I scrubbed in wonder, my heart soaring with the truth of it. How could my reluctant service to this elderly aunt have produced in my heart a truly warm, sacrificial love for her? My memory paraded short incidents, accumulated over time: my playfully snatching a billowing sheet out of her feeble grasp when she repeatedly tried to help me make her bed; the twenty-year stash of presents under every bed and in every closet waiting to be regifted; the rare peach-colored iris bulbs she had given me from her own garden. Over time, mutual tolerance had blossomed into genuine regard, then something altogether lovelier. With that thought, I scrubbed a little more zealously, wanting to show her just how much I truly loved her by scrubbing out her weakness.

At that precise moment, the Lord revealed the real lesson. With a single piercing flash, I came to understand that he felt the same way about those "disgusting" church members I longed to scrub out of our church as I felt about Aunt Betty. Their profound weakness moved him to love them desperately, for he knew full well that only he could ever help them, and only he longed to do so. Above all, I understood in a way that changed me permanently that "mercy triumphs over judgment" (Jas 2:13).

I wept at the foot of her toilet in the Pepto-Bismol pink bathroom with the shiny silver swans on the wallpaper and the mauve shag carpet, like I had never wept before. His mercy had brought me out of the same rebellion they were in, corrected me, and placed me on the right path. His mercy preserved a cynical Aunt Betty to be a witness of his love, and his mercy showed me how to love those church members and treat them with the charity for which they were created.

I was made aware, in the deepest seat of my soul, that the weakness in myself that I abhor so desperately, the weakness that provokes all my defenses and denial and pretension, the neediness I hide, is always what draws the Lord closest to me. Clinging to this knowledge, I am increasingly able to beg for grace whenever this weakness is triggered by a hateful "other," and I am suddenly called to control my own instinctive incontinence.

"Who is weak, and I am not weak? Who is made to fall, and I am not indignant? . . . 'For power is made perfect in weakness.' So I will boast all the more gladly of my weaknesses, so that the power of Christ may rest upon in me" (2 Cor 11:29, 12:9). Seen in this light, our most painful shame becomes the path on which we soar to sanctity. The crusty old woman and our nasty Christian sister and brother become the sweetest allies, our personal escorts to holiness.

Let's Review

Let's review how God unleashes us through our relationship patterns:

Relationships are difficult, but God wants to grow sacrificial love in us through them.

God, himself, exists in perfect life-giving relationship, so all my relationships and their health are important to him.

The Holy Spirit works through, not despite, my own personality and all the personalities around me.

God uses certain types of people to draw my hurts and wounds and memories to the surface so he can heal them. I will probably be drawn to these people, especially in my vocation.

God unleashes me through my vocation, unto a relationship with him.

There is a memory associated with every emotional eruption. If I can fully feel the emotions of that memory in God's presence and work through it with him, he can heal it forever and it will have no other power over me.

Family relationships and people in my church can both instill and trigger my hurts and wounds. God uses these times to help me grow in charity and heal me.

My neighbor's irritating behavior is a mirror that shows me where God wants to unleash my life.

When God speaks to *me, he is speaking* about *me.*

I must forgive in order to be forgiven.

An Invitation

Regarding my relationship with my father, there were many memories that had to be confronted and felt. I can always trace back to this root my temptations toward my predominant fault in my relationships. Once I recognize it as "my Daddy thing," it no longer has power over me, and I am

invited to practice charity in my relationships. What relationship pattern(s) has this chapter led you to recall in your
own life, which point to a need for deeper healing?

Once we are unleashed by the power of forgiveness from the wounds of the past, the cycle of wounding
and hurting can be broken—although you may find that
some of the damage has already been done and needs to
be addressed in the same way. For example, when I was
unleashed from my relationship wounds from my father, I
began dealing with his interactions with my sons. I had to
put some boundaries in place regarding my kids' relationship with my father, too, but I understood that as far as it
was possible, I needed to cultivate a good relationship for
all of our sakes.

> If possible, so far as it depends on you, live peace-
> ably with all. Beloved, never avenge yourselves,
> but leave room for the wrath of God; for it is
> written, "Vengeance is mine, I will repay, says
> the Lord." No, "if your enemies are hungry, feed
> them; if they are thirsty, give them something to
> drink; for by doing this you will heap burning
> coals on their heads." Do not be overcome by evil,
> but overcome evil with good. (Rom 12:18–21)

Are you struggling to find a way to rebuild a relationship with someone—assuming it is safe for you to continue
in relationship with him or her—or even to forgive that person? Let me suggest a simple exercise that helped me.

In the process of seeking to reconcile with my dad, God
had me make a list of all the good things I could think of
about him. I realized, and was even embarrassed by, how
often I focused on the negatives. By recognizing the gifts of
the other person, however unwanted those gifts may be at
times, we continue to walk the way of peace as much for
our own sakes as theirs.

And so, as you continue that walk of peace, consider: what act of charity, however small, can you offer to God regarding the relationship or pattern of relationships you brought to him through this chapter?

God Prompt

Deep within the soul, in every soul, there is something that gets entombed, messed up, confused, and perverted by what has happened to us. Childhood pain in my relationship with my father made me afraid, rebellious, and angry. Early emotional confusion led to insecurities, projections, difficulties, and negative emotions in my relationships with men in every area of my life. I was one of *those* people with a chip on my shoulder and an epithet in my mouth. I was in pain. Are you in pain? Has someone wounded you very deeply?

The first exercise I was called to after discerning my relationship pattern with men in authority and the painful memories associated with my pattern was forgiveness. Did you know the Bible says that we cannot be forgiven if we do not forgive? Forgiveness does not mean the other person is innocent of wrongdoing. It just means you leave thoughts and actions of revenge and punishment and outcomes to God where the other person is concerned. For big hurts, forgiveness is rarely a one-time occurrence; it must be repeated every time a memory or emotion is triggered.

In order to help me recognize and move past my lack of forgiveness, God invited me to call my father and ask him to forgive me for the rudeness and disrespect with which I treated him before our three-year estrangement. I was devastated and felt completely betrayed. What I know now is that in almost every conflict I have with another person, there is *something* I can take responsibility and apologize for, and often that small act of true sacrifice will change the situation for the better immediately. But when God first asked me to take this step, I felt as if he was sweeping all my hurts under the rug and blaming me for them, rather than the person responsible.

Only after months of hostility and skepticism was I able to accept God's suggestion to call my dad, and when I did, he blamed me for the whole episode. But alleluia! Like an invisible, connecting string popping loose, I was free of his painful hold over me from that day forward—by some crazy, invisible miracle of grace—and I realized with awe that that was the reason my Heavenly Father had asked me to do it all along.

Through all my relationships God specifically allows repeated provocation of my most painful, negative feelings; he purposely allows the infliction of my greatest pains, in order to point out *my* faults and weaknesses. Continually, he invites me to work with him to continue rooting out and unleashing me from my faults and weaknesses.

Dear One, your relationship patterns reveal another area where God has been working to unleash you and is already at work. He wants you to join him there. If you do and persevere with him, you will stop repeating those relationships that suck the life out of you. He did it for me, and he is still doing it.

Maybe it's a spouse, a coworker, a church or family member. In some area of your life, is there a particular person, or type of person, whom you simply cannot tolerate, someone who consistently brings out the very worst behaviors and judgments or the most painful emotions in you? Is there someone with whom you seem in constant conflict with, if only internally? What if God wants to teach you something through the living flame of this person or type of person? What if he wants to unleash something in you, or something in them, through this relationship, and whisper something to you about yourself?

We often do not consider this possibility, because we can only see their faults. Relationships are designed to grow us, but most often we concentrate so vigorously on others' faults that we are unable to receive the lesson whispered to us through them. Although notoriously true in family, it is also true in the "family of God" and in all our relationships.

Attempt to discern the relationship pattern: Has the Holy Spirit spoken to you through this chapter about your relationship patterns?

Did a particular relationship come to mind as you read? What is the primary fault you discern in this person?

Try to name the strongest emotion that surfaces as you think of this person and your interactions with him or her.

Probe for the self-knowledge: Remembering that the Holy Spirit is here with you, repeat the verses in this passage before him, maybe even emphasizing each phrase in turn. Ask him what he would like to reveal to you through the relationship he brought to mind.

> Do not judge, so that you may not be judged. For with the judgment you make you will be judged, and the measure you give will be the measure you get. Why do you see the speck in your neighbor's eye, but do not notice the log in your own eye? Or how can you say to your neighbor, "Let me take the speck out of your eye," when there is the log in your own eye? You hypocrite, first take the log out of your own eye, and then you will see clearly to take the speck out of your neighbor's eye. (Mt 7:1–5)

I can always tell I am judging rather than making an observation by the air of disdain and criticism that creeps in. As you spend some time evaluating the relationship in God's presence, do you have the same basic fault or weakness in an area of your own life?

Does this shared fault or weakness affect your life in any way?

Attempt to discern the memory rooted in the relationship:
Do your best to name your worst relationship pattern or
habit.

In God's presence and remembering that he holds you
in his heart and protective hands, think about the emotion
triggered by this particular relationship pattern. Is it particularly strong, an eruption? Would you say this emotion is the
product of some past relationship hurt or historical emotion?
Do you have a memory or series of memories associated
with this particular person or emotion?

When you are able to, privately talk to God about all
the circumstances of this relationship pattern and pour out
all the feelings involved. Gathering and articulating may
take considerable time, but please do not rush. Try very
hard not to numb the pain; the feelings must be completely
remembered to be completely eradicated.

Try to articulate the need: God created us to need. We are
needy and weak by design. *Neediness is not a fault or sin*, even
though it feels awful. See if you can identify the prevailing
motivation behind your relationship pattern. In other words,
what do or did you need from this relationship or pattern of
relationships that you do not or did not receive?

How often would you say your relationship pattern
could be narrowed down to this prevailing need?

Remembering that he is your provider, pour out the
whole truth to God about your needs and ask him to provide
for them, especially your need for comfort. It may take time
for him to work, but try very hard not to self-medicate while
you wait on him to provide.

From now on: When I get that disturbed feeling in my
stomach and heart after an interaction with another person,
this is the process I go through to determine the root of the
internal battle. What feelings have been provoked? What
faults do I see in them? What truth does God want to whisper to me about myself through this exchange?

5

*W*hy Do You Call Me "Lord, Lord" but Not Do What I Command?

Luke 6:46, NAB

Catching the Lessons God Most Wants to Teach Us

I am a legend. My fame as a motor-vehicle operator is a well-known fact to my neighbors, friends, and extended family. My neighbors for miles all did drive-bys several years ago when they heard the fire trucks screaming at my house. I had blown up my husband's cherished '78 Ford four-by-four when I tried to start it after he had removed the carburetor. Hey, who knew?

It was the windiest day on record for years, so the truck was engulfed in flames, high enough to be seen ten miles away, faster than I could open the hood. I should warn you

95

that an under-the-counter kitchen fire extinguisher can't put a dent in a gas fire. We live so far out in the country that the fire trucks arrived after the tires exploded. The firemen just shook their heads. I went without eyebrows for weeks.

It wasn't the first time I'd had a falling-out with a piece of machinery. Another time a riding lawn mower with a sticky gear shift somehow landed upside down at the bottom of our creek while under my control. I thought it was in reverse, so I gunned the accelerator to back away from the edge of the creek bank. Instead, I found myself soaring over the bank while negotiating an awkward leap off the back of the mower. I did manage to avoid being pinned to the creek bed, but I walked home dripping algae and fish water with a crayfish clinging to my shirt tail.

My husband and son have been known to regale our family and friends as well as total strangers with tales of my, uh, difficulties. With great comedic detail, they recall the time when my oldest son was three and told my husband that policemen give mama "mail" through her car window. At eleven, the same son asked my father, a retired state patrolman, why he stopped at the stop sign at the end of our road since I never did. My family insists they've worn out the grip handles in my car.

Somehow this stuff always gets brought up at our family gatherings. "Remember the time Sonja was distracted by buzzards and lost the fender splash guard in a ditch?" The very next day my husband came home with it. (How in the world could he have spotted it? How did he even know it was mine?) Or, "Remember the time Sonja ran into a boat somebody parked 'surreptitiously' right behind her car?" I didn't think I hurt anything so I didn't mention it. But when my husband came home early from a fishing trip right after that, I wondered if the leak that had almost sunk his boat was my fault. We laugh till we cry, because everyone knows I get it from my mother, who gets it from hers!

When we first moved to the country, I got three speeding tickets in one year, but only because the highway is like an interstate out here. Because I am a firm believer in justice, I have never tried to get out of a speeding ticket, and have, therefore, been to traffic school five times for tickets in two counties and two states. Which, if you think about it, is pretty surprising, given that my father was a career state patrolman, and I know exactly how many miles an hour over the speed limit I can drive without being ticketed, and many other useful items of safety trivia.

After that I decided to set my cruise control on every major highway and drive to town exclusively on back roads whenever I could. Even those precautions didn't save me: not long after, I saw lights in my rearview window, a city cop who had been hiding behind the rise of a hill, holding a radar gun on a lightly traveled back road. I prayed for another warning, but not nearly as hard as I thanked God that my sons were not in the car to tell on me when I got home. So you can imagine my bewilderment when I found myself signing yet another little piece of mail pushed through the car window. God's will was clear: I needed to slow down.

How many times has God attempted to correct this undisciplined and even dangerous behavior in my life? I know the answer is many times—many tickets, many warnings, many trips to traffic school that kept our insurance rates from ballooning, many jokes and sideways glances regarding my driving. The truth of this embarrasses and shames me.

As I drove away from the scene of the crime, the Lord asked me if something awful would have to happen before I finally took the issue seriously. It is a testament to his grace and patience that he has protected me and my family for so long while I laughed away this glaring lack of discipline and self-control. What a horrible example of how I practice my faith. What is more, God was not laughing. I noticed the call to repentance in the readings the days before and after the ticket: "Why do you call me 'Lord' but not do what I command?" (Lk 6:46).

"Harmless" Sin?

Is there some continuing circumstance you laugh off as just a quirk of your personality? Has God attempted, repeatedly, to speak to you through your circumstances about something you consider trivial?

My husband has always been the one to suffer most from my negligence. He has spent a lot of precious free time repairing damage I have caused, pulling the mower out of the creek and water out of its motor, towing away the burned-out skeleton of a beloved truck, finding a place in the budget for court costs and traffic school, sending up prayers when I travel to my parents' with the kids and worrying anxiously till we get home.

In my twenties I struggled to change the communication in my marriage, frustrations in my relationships with my parents and sibling, my difficulties at work, my own bad habits—but all my labor seemed to make everything worse. I prayed with weeping and gnashing of teeth (Mt 13:42), but God never seemed to answer my prayers for substantial change.

Do you pray and pray again about your circumstances, asking God to change them, and nothing happens? When God does not improve our circumstances, what if it's because he wants to improve us instead? Aren't our circumstances a series of attempts by God to get our attention? To us they may seem arbitrary, but according to the mystics, the intent is to order all our suffering toward the maximization of our potential so that our suffering ultimately contributes to our salvation.

Jesus told us something we seem to rarely believe: "In the world you will have tribulation. But be of good cheer; I have overcome the world" (Jn 16:33). The word *tribulation* means "pressure, affliction, burden, pain, trouble, problem." What if God is working to unleash an area of my life and attempting to teach me something whenever I am experiencing any of these? I said we rarely believe we will (or should) suffer, because the way we react to problems and difficulties indicates that we think it's abnormal. I throw fits, get angry, bawl, pout, or rebel.

How do you tend to react to pressures, afflictions, burdens, pain troubles, and problems? How do you feel? Do you usually react outwardly, in aggression, or inwardly, in suppression? Our instinctive reactions to suffering tell us important things about ourselves.

> Come to me, all who labor and are heavy laden, and I will give you rest. Take my yoke upon you, and learn from me; for I am gentle and lowly in heart, and you will find rest for your souls. For my yoke is easy, and my burden is light. (Mt 11:28–30)

Jesus promises us rest in the midst of our burdens, but this is not what we usually experience when in the throes of tribulation.

The Yoke of Suffering

A *yoke* was a valuable, heavy piece of farm equipment, so heavy it required two oxen to carry it and steer and operate the plow. The farmer always placed a new ox with an older, more experienced ox. New oxen go too fast or slow, in turn pulling at and resisting the unfamiliar, uncomfortably heavy yoke. When a new ox resists the old ox's rhythm and experience, they plow crooked rows that are too deep or too shallow for seed.

Consider the yoke spoken of in this passage as trials and tribulation. Jesus says the burden should not be difficult or heavy. If it is, am I resisting the yoke and pulling against the plow intended to prepare the soil for seed? Jesus seems to say I can submit to the yoke, yield control, take it on myself willingly, and learn from him, for he is gentle and humble of heart; under his yoke, with his help and experience, I can learn exactly how to carry it, and there, under the yoke, I can find rest from runaway emotions.

Because of childhood experiences, pain became synonymous with punishment for me. I used to think God was punishing me in times of lack, afflictions, and pain. I endured this warped sense of God until one day I just asked him if I was in trouble. I will never forget how it felt to hear him gently speak to my heart and say, "Dearest Child, if you are 'in trouble,' I will certainly tell you." Do you know, through all my sin and waywardness and stumbling, he has never told me I was in trouble?

Since then, I have learned it is I who resist the yoke of my circumstances. Don't all of us chafe under pain and difficulty? We don't seem to know any better. The most natural reaction to pain is to flee. Yet avoidance of pain and suffering is an avoidance of truth. If I can submit to the painful circumstance, I might hear God speak through it.

Jesus spoke about a common reaction to pain in Matthew 13:20–21. He taught that those who have no spiritual roots "fall away" when the inevitable tribulation comes. To *fall away* is also translated as "offended" and literally means "enticed to sin." Instead, Jesus models a proper understanding of suffering in Luke 9:51: "When the days drew near for him to be taken up, he set his face to go to Jerusalem." Jesus was not merely willing, he was determined to suffer when it was clearly in the line of duty.

The word *suffer* in the scriptures literally means "passion." Jesus' crown of suffering is called his "Passion" by the Church, but not because he celebrated, kicking up his heels and rejoicing all the way to Jerusalem. He asked to be delivered. He sweated blood. His soul was troubled (Jn 12:27).

Over and over the scriptures give witness to how deliberate Jesus was in his purpose to accept suffering—not just any suffering, but rejection by his own Jewish brothers and crucifixion by infidel Gentiles. Besides redemption for us, God was accomplishing something else in Jesus, something we all share. Jesus was learning obedience (Heb 5:8).

In addition to merely doing what one is told, scriptural use of the term *obedience* carries emphatic connotations of hearing. Jesus learned *to hear* God through the things he suffered. Can we also learn to hear God through those things we suffer?

We see that pain and suffering are in the normal pattern of growth, and that avoidance causes sickness or sin. C. S. Lewis once said God shouts in our pains. "Pain is God's megaphone to rouse a deaf world."[1] And so it is. It teaches us to hear without the noise of words.

St. Peter tells us pain and suffering is cleansing. Those who willingly accept this important function of suffering experience something utterly astounding: "Since therefore Christ suffered in the flesh, arm yourselves with the same thought, for whoever has suffered in the flesh has *ceased from sin, so as to live for the rest of the time in the flesh no longer by human passions* but by the will of God." (1 Pt 4:1–2, emphasis added). What a stunning statement. Human passions include emotional binges and out-of-control emotions that accompany problems, tribulations and trials, suffering and pain.

Rather than God's getting even with us for sin, suffering is his tool to actively purify us of it, teaching us how, through what we suffer, to hear his voice, and to choose the good. As our awkward ears become attuned to hear, we discover something utterly remarkable: that everything that ever happens in our adult lives can be the most perfect thing possibly arranged for our good by Benevolence and

Love Itself, especially those things that cause us the most pain, for they can unleash us and unleash God within us.

But does God unleash us only through negative circumstances? Could he also be whispering through our positive ones too? In the Old Testament, the story of Joseph taught me something really neat about how God uses circumstances to unleash his people.

Twice Makes a Pattern

Several months ago, a woman approached me at a conference, handed me a rose, and said something wonderful but weirdly prophetic sounding. I don't usually put much stock in things like that, but shortly afterward, another woman handed me a second rose and thanked me for my "Unleashed" talk. I'm no prophet, but I have learned through discerning my patterns that when I see or hear something two or more times, I can be sure God is about to unleash something into my life. I had no clue what it all meant, however. I thought I would just wait and see.

Not long after that occurrence, I was watching a rainstorm from my porch when a rainbow appeared. Rainbows have always been sort of an inside thing for me and God, so I found it interesting. As I watched, a second rainbow appeared beside the first. I got chills. What in the world, if anything, did it mean?

At the time, I was writing a Bible study on biblical heroes of faith. What I discovered there was not a simple answer but a real unleashing of his word.

When God wants to save the world he chooses someone through whom to do it. Isn't that an incredible thought? He used a double dream to choose Joseph, who is called a hero of faith in Hebrews 11, the main text of the study I was writing. Twice, Joseph dreamed he would become superior in prominence over his father and eleven brothers. In the culture of his day, the firstborn was the prominent one. Joseph's dreams pictured the primacy he would eventually possess in the family. Joseph's dreams not only insulted his older brothers and father; they violated custom.

Back in Joseph's day, visions and dreams were important. In Egypt and Mesopotamia the science of dream interpretation was a highly developed skill. An Egyptian papyrus that dates back to 1300 BC details dream interpretation. Joseph's father Jacob was one whose life had been changed by a dream of a ladder with angels ascending and descending its rungs. God gave two dreams to the youngest son of the covenant family. The brothers were so offended that they intended to kill him, but instead that they sold Joseph into slavery out of convenience.

Joseph learned important lessons in discernment, as we're all invited to, through his sufferings and difficulties as a slave in Egypt. A false accusation landed him in Pharaoh's dungeon, but he quickly rose to prominence there too. Talk about patterns in difficult circumstances.

As a trustee of the prison, Joseph served whatever high officials were under house arrest awaiting the disposition of the charges against them. Joseph was in the dungeon with Pharaoh's butler and baker, important officers in the royal court who had gotten into some sort of hot water. Another double dream occurred one night when the butler and baker each had a dream. Joseph was not only a dreamer but could also interpret dreams; his interpretation of both men's dreams came to pass. The butler was executed and the baker was released the next day.

After suffering two more long years in the dungeon, another double dream occurred. Now Pharaoh was dreaming. The dream was distressing to him because he experienced it twice in varying forms that were interrupted by waking. The meaning was a puzzle, because seven lean cows remained lean and gaunt even after consuming seven fat cattle. The same was true with stalks of grain. Although it was abnormal for cows to eat cows or grain to consume grain, surely the lean things should have grown fatter by all they ate. Something had to be wrong, but what was it?

The king's usual source of such information was the magicians, but they were totally baffled, as was Pharaoh. They were the wisest, best-educated men of Pharaoh's kingdom, schooled in the art of dream interpretation. But only Joseph, relying on God, could fathom the meaning of the dreams. Pharaoh was so impressed with Joseph, that he made him administrator of the entire kingdom, second only to Pharaoh himself. About seven years later, Joseph's brothers bowed before him. Joseph's dreams had come true.

The sentence that leaped off the page as I considered how to write the Bible study lesson was from Joseph's interpretation of Pharaoh's dreams: "And the doubling of Pharoah's dream means that the thing is fixed by God, and God will shortly bring it about" (Gn 41:32). I realized the doubling of the roses and rainbows meant the same thing. About a week later, the woman's prediction came true and I was invited to write this very book. The Holy Spirit was unleashed at my conference talk, through my Bible study time, and through all my circumstances. He actually told me the future and brought it to pass. Utterly astounding.

What if he is doing the same for you?

Certainly, not every circumstance that occurs twice is the action of God. But I do not believe much in coincidences. How can I know the difference without seeing signs in every experience? Like Jesus, I must first learn to hear God speak through my difficult circumstances. Once I learn to discern his voice from the others competing for my attention, I can know if he is unleashing something into my life or if he's simply attempting to get my attention.

Let's Review

Let's review how God unleashes us within and through our circumstances:

> *The Holy Spirit repeatedly attempts to correct me* through my circumstances.
>
> *Some circumstances can grow more and more painful* the longer I fail to hear the message in them.
>
> *Every human being will experience terrible pain and problems,* but suffering can contribute to my salvation.
>
> *I can learn to hear God through my suffering* if I can submit to painful circumstances, just like Jesus did.
>
> *If I experience something twice or more,* I should pay attention.
>
> *I should wait to discern if God is speaking, and see if he confirms it,* especially through the scriptures.

An Invitation

Have you seen the movie *Castaway* in which Tom Hanks plays a man who becomes the sole survivor of a plane crash? He winds up on a deserted island, where he has to survive for months on the few supplies he can gather.

Now, imagine for a moment that you are in a similar situation—perhaps a sinking ship—from which you managed to salvage a bit of fuel with a few other provisions. For weeks you eke out an existence, until at last a ship appears on the horizon. Hastily you build a signal fire, pouring the last remnants of fuel upon it, to signal the ship.

But all in vain. The ship sails past.

Worse still, you discover you were a little too generous with the fuel oil. The fire gets out of control. Sparks fly onto the roof of your hut. In what seems like a few moments, everything you own, the few supplies on which you depend for survival, has been consumed by a raging inferno.

All is lost. Without those essentials you won't survive. Suddenly you see that the ship, which had earlier passed by, is now heading in your direction!

Once you are finally on board, you find the captain to thank him and to ask him the one question you have been waiting anxiously to ask: "What made you turn around when you had already passed me by?"

"Why," explains the captain, "we saw that impressive signal fire. Setting your hut on fire—that was good thinking!"

Over and over, when I have asked God why certain things happened, he has been faithful to point out patterns in my circumstances that shed light on that question, even if I did not get a direct answer. "Why?" may be an impossible question for him to answer for me right away, but he always gives me something in the meantime. I believe God wants us to know far more about what he is up to in our lives than we could even imagine. Dear One, the patterns in your circumstances reveal where God has been working to unleash you from something.

Believe that he is already at work—and that he wants you to join him.

If you do and persevere with him, suffering, pain, and troubles will do their work in purifying your heart and sharpening your discernment. Then you will begin to notice all the wonderful little surprise packages he has been sending you all along.

So from now on, anytime you experience a painful circumstance, especially more than once, begin looking for signs of God's activity. What do the daily readings say? Journaling is particularly helpful for discernment over a longer period of time. I often find God has been speaking through the scriptures and my circumstances over a whole week or more. Don't forget to anticipate those pop quizzes this week and anytime God is teaching you something.

Finally, pay attention to your dreams: I'm not going to get all new agey on you, but ask any psychologist and she will tell you that because dreams are a mechanism by which the subconscious processes experiences, conflicts, fears, and concerns, they are useful for mental health and emotional and spiritual evaluation. They are a little like truth-telling personal letters that reveal things we might otherwise ignore, deny, or seem not to know. Without our dreams we would all be crazy and even physically unhealthy.

It is by the sense of their work in favor of our health and well-being that we can consider dreams to be "from God" without descending into new ageism, delusion, or superstition. With that qualification in mind, consider writing out the account of a dream that you particularly remember, one that you feel was a message from God or was otherwise somehow prophetic, and especially any reoccurring dream you may have. Spend some time researching dream symbols, and see if you learn anything about yourself or the dream.

God Prompt

Have you ever been in the middle of a tragic or confusing circumstance where, in your prayers, you accused God of things you knew were not true of him? Perhaps you have said, "God does not love me," or "He just wants to hurt or control me." When I am unsure what the Holy Spirit is doing or saying, I pray this passage:

> Consider it all joy, my brothers, when you encounter various trials, for you know that the testing of your faith produces perseverance. And let perseverance be perfect, so that you may be perfect and complete, lacking in nothing. *But if any of you lacks*

*wisdom, he should ask God who gives to all generously
and ungrudgingly, and he will be given it.* (Jas 1:2–5,
NAB, emphasis added)

From a biblical perspective, wisdom means to see things
the way God sees them. To understand my painful or difficult circumstances, God's perspective is vital, and this verse
promises that he will give it to me. In fact, it is impossible to
determine the truth of a situation until I have heard the truth
from God. I can ask, and wait; I can adjust my life to what he
is accomplishing by doing all he tells me to do. That's when
I experience God's shocking, saving, healing unleashing in
my life and circumstances.

When I am confused by my circumstances, I remember
this promise and ask God to reveal his intents and purposes,
his wisdom.

Can you see yourself as the recipient of this promise?
Notice your reaction to the passage. What might the Holy
Spirit be whispering to you?

Attempt to discern the pattern in your circumstances: Has
the Holy Spirit spoken to you through this chapter about
any of your circumstances? Did a particular experience or
series of similar experiences come to mind as you read?
What is the primary lesson you can discern from this circumstance or pattern? Try to name the strongest emotion
that surfaces as you think of possible patterns in things you
have experienced.

Probe for the self-knowledge: You may want to light a
candle, do a breathing exercise to recollect yourself, or put
on your favorite sacred music. Perhaps you prefer silence.
Remembering that the Holy Spirit is here with you, ask him
if he has been attempting to get your attention through your
circumstances. Spend some time talking to him about your
worries and concerns. Sit quietly and listen, letting your
mind wander where it may. What comes to mind? What
might he want to share with you about that?

Attempt to discern his voice: Remember that God speaks and brings order and light through the scriptures. Do your best to obtain today's Office of Readings. If you do not have a breviary, Laudate or other app, or one of the little magazines like *Magnificat, Give Us This Day*, or *Word Among Us*, some websites that have the Office of Readings are easily available: apostleshipofprayer.org, universalis.com, usccb.org, and ewtn.com. Remembering your conversation with the Lord in the previous exercise, read through at least the gospel reading for today. You may want to read it more than once. Does any word or phrase particularly strike you? What is God saying to you? Could he be offering you an answer to your prayer? Don't forget to thank him for that answer—including not only his response to your prayers right now, but all the answers he will show you in the future. That kind of faith is irresistible to God!

6

*D*o You Love Me?

John 21:16

Chasing the Desires That Lead to God

The car was mostly packed, almost ready for our trip to Disney World. Someone with small hands had gotten bleach on a bath towel; I don't remember if it was my sister or me. But my dad asked us, then six and ten years old or so, who had done it, and since one of us had to have done it, one of us lied. Or maybe we honestly didn't know. Dad was furious, both at the ruined towel and our denials.

My parents went inside to get the luggage and finish loading the car while my sister and I waited breathlessly in our seats, wriggling and noisy like a couple of excited puppies. They probably weren't inside long, but it felt like forever. I reached up and beeped the horn, and we never went to Disney World, ever.

When I was ten I dreamed of getting a ten-speed bike. I asked for it all year. We had recently moved, and because there was lots of pavement, the location was better for bicycle riding than anywhere we had ever lived. I couldn't wait to get it and hardly slept that Christmas Eve. When I got up and opened all my presents, I was confused. They were wonderful, but there was no ten-speed. I had had behavior and other problems at school that year, and my dad felt I hadn't deserved it. I was crushed.

In the gospels, we find that Peter experienced the same thing after his failure. We see it in his tears and, later, in his encounter with Jesus after the Great Denial. I wonder what Peter's greatest desire in life was?

Peter was the one who risked articulating Jesus' true identity on behalf of the other disciples (Mt 16:16). Peter was the one who jumped out of the boat in a storm and walked on water (Mt 14:29). Peter was the one who dared rebuke the Lord (Mt 16:22). Peter wept uncontrollably after betraying Jesus (Mt 26:75). Peter jumped into the water fully clothed to meet Jesus on the shore after the Resurrection (Jn 21:7). Peter risked it all, all the time.

Presumptuous and impetuous? Absolutely. But the Holy Spirit works with our personalities and temperaments, because he made them for a purpose. I bet Peter's greatest longing was for leadership and greatness, because that's what Jesus said he would exemplify. How devastated Peter must have been when Jesus looked him in the eye as he denied him three times. Surely his designation as the leader, the rock, was all over. Of course Jesus would retract the gift he had given Peter, his call to lead. He deserved it, after all. True, true.

And yet, I can't think of a more devastating occurrence, than for Jesus to purposely withhold what he had already said was mine because I was "bad." What a penetrating question: "Do you love me?" How embarrassing and heartbreaking to be asked three times in front of the people you were once supposed to lead. It seems cruel and purposely hurtful, yet every time, Jesus publicly reconfirmed Peter's call: "Feed my lambs. . . . Tend my sheep" (Jn 21:15–17).

Why doesn't Jesus retract his call to Peter when Peter clearly seemed to forfeit it? Partly, because he repented, I am sure, but also because "the gifts and the call of God are irrevocable" (Rom 11:29). I just know Peter desired nothing more than to do all Jesus called him to do.

Maybe it's just me, but I think desire is one of the things folks tend to be most dishonest about, both with themselves and other people. Perhaps it's because desire can be a little tyrant that reveals I'm merely mortal after all, one not especially enlightened besides, who is too insignificant and unformed herself to stand in the front of the room and articulate any pretty philosophy for life. Because they are often banshees and drunken monkeys, dark and mysterious, and originate from who knows where, desires are powerful. Desires "form the passageway and ensure the connection between the life of the senses and the life of the mind" (CCC 1764). A scattered or dispersed desire is one focused on something other than love. An unacknowledged or scattered desire is a dangerous spiritual enemy, one that lies beneath all of the world's worst injustices.

Isn't the dark side of desire fear, fear my desire is too tall an order, or that it might possess and devour me? Part of the negative residue of my childhood and religious tradition was the development of a deep-seated suspicion that if I wanted something a whole lot, it was probably bad for me, and even if it wasn't, I wasn't good enough to have it anyway. Even then I believed everything that happened to me was God's will, and it all usually seemed to include punishment and the denial of what I wanted.

The day I married I stood in the back of the church in my wedding dress, absolutely positive that there would be a massive earthquake and the ground would open up and swallow me before I could get my "I do" said. Wonderful things seemed always just beyond my grasp. I was afraid to want anything too much.

Is Desire Bad?

Here's a thought: what if our desires are meant to lead us to God? "The . . . natural desire for happiness . . . is of divine origin: God has placed it in the human heart in order to draw man to the One who alone can fulfill it . . ." (CCC 1718). Truly, we have all experienced how desire can become disordered, controlling, and even evil. But isn't that usually because we are untrained in discerning what it is we truly desire under the surface? My strong desire to marry and have a family originated from God, who plans to sanctify and lead me to himself through my husband and family. My desire can lead me to God. What is it we always ultimately desire?

Does the man really desire to watch porn, or does he do it because sex and love are wired together in his brain and he is longing for intimacy? Does the woman with same-sex attraction simply want sterile sex, or is she expressing an unmet need for affirmation, nurturing, and love? Does the addict really desire to have that next hangover, or does the substance cover shame and feelings of worthlessness by stimulating the pleasure centers of the brain associated with love and happiness? Does the teenaged girl really desire to get pregnant, or does she simply yearn for someone to love her totally and unconditionally?

"'I want to see God' expresses the true desire of man" (CCC 2557). As limited creatures with an unlimited capacity for love, we perpetually deny and mask our truest yearnings because they are our most terrifying, gaping, vulnerable spots. Desires are profound and they matter a lot, a whole lot, and we are scared to death we might never possess what we want and need most. There have been times my desires felt so miserable and indiscernible I had no idea what I needed; I just felt restless and unfulfilled. But the husband of my soul knows. God always knows, and only he can discern and touch that deeply. Have I asked him to?

The Holy Spirit Can Integrate Desire

The mystics spoke of intense desires, or passions, a lot. The Church calls scattered or disordered desires *concupiscence*. The mystery of sin makes the natural inclination of human desire tend toward disorder. Concupiscence is the downward drag of impulses we inadequately control.

> Etymologically [the origin of the word], "concupiscence" can refer to any intense form of human desire. Christian theology has given it a particular meaning: the movement of the sensitive appetite [longing of the senses] contrary to the operation of the human reason. . . . [Concupiscence] is a consequence of sin and at the same time a confirmation of it. (CCC 2515–16)

Because the tendency toward disorder leads our natural desires astray and draws us away from God and toward destruction, desires often get a bad rap.

Sex is perhaps the most disordered passion of our time. "Sexual pleasure is morally disordered when sought for itself, isolated from its procreative and unitive purposes" (CCC 2351). But don't we all *need* touch, intimacy, permanent love? Is it healthy or happy to pretend physical desire and need isn't there? If you are in a season of life, an orientation, or vocation in which sex is illicit, can't wrestling with the desire and frustration of your status draw you to God?

The bigger question might be: *Can physical desire lead me to God?* As a non-Catholic all I knew was the spiritual aspect of faith. I remember telling God, "I wish there was some way we could be *closer!*" Primarily, I meant physically. When my sister was small she went to my mother, scared after a bad dream. Mom told her to pray to God, and my sister said, "I need somebody with skin on them!" That's a little like how I felt. I thought of this closeness in nuptial terms. I thought it was impossible.

The Incarnation affirms the beauty of our creation as physical *and* spiritual creatures. We were created to be sensual beings. The Church, through the grace of the Holy Spirit unleashed in her at Pentecost, has been so wise to retain the sensual aspects of worship—kneelers, incense, candles, music, the Eucharistic bread and wine as Body and Blood—because it all engages us through the senses.

When I received my first Eucharist, it was with complete awe that he had answered my prayer for us to somehow be closer and had touched and satisfied my deepest desire in every possible way—physically, emotionally, intellectually, and spiritually. Physically receiving him truly felt like a supermarital moment, in part because I longed for it so desperately.

What do I desire physically? What are my emotional needs and wants? What do I hope for intellectually? What are my spiritual desires?

Finding the Ground of the Soul

In your world, what do you desire—right now, this year, for the rest of your life? Be specific. Perhaps just the question has every desire you've ever entertained surfacing, leaping out of the water like spawning salmon. You may answer: "I want a bag of potato chips." And maybe that's true on the surface. But what's under that desire? Are you hungry, bored, or sad? Can a bag of chips relieve any of those deeper longings? Why are you bored? Why are you sad?

Maybe the first question is, *What do I really want?* But to get deeper and know what we yearn for, we have to keep asking *why* till we get all the way to the bottom of the desire. It's very important to know what a true desire is, because that may actually be what God desires for us.

"Take delight in the Lord, and he will give you the desires of your heart" (Ps 37:4). Does this verse mean God will give us desires or that he will fulfill them? I believe it's both. I believe all my deepest, truest desires come from him. I believe God waits and searches for those who have and pursue dreams and desires that are too big for them, just to show how big his love is.

I have pursued God my whole life, and I know when my intense desires have taken a detour to Mordor. Why do I want to eat too much, drink too much, work too much, or yell too much? Do I *need* that pair of shoes or am I bored? I don't always deny such desires, but if they begin to slide into habits, I start looking for why, because I know such habits zap my spiritual potency and leave me emptier than before.

When I get to the ground of a scattered or disordered desire, I find what I am truly yearning for. Then I ask God for it, because I also know he is simply waiting to knock my socks off. "No eye has seen, nor ear heard, nor the heart of man conceived, what God has prepared for those who love him" (1 Cor 2:9). Unless you are truly motivated by vile ambitions, your desires are moving you toward a holier, more unleashed, integrated, and healthy you. My truest desires will always lead me to what is good for me.

Go Big or Go Home

When I did all I could and entreated him to do the rest—the big stuff—I have seen God unleash in my own life, in every area I dared invite him, to accomplish my deepest, strongest

desires. Isn't it better to want a truly happy marriage, and
spiritually and emotionally healthy children, rather than
just look like I do? Won't I go further in my growth and
development if I pursue education for the sake of learning
more than to guarantee a lucrative job? Won't I be healthier
and happier surrounded by intimacy and love than to climb
some social or financial ladder? Is it living to ignore that
dream I had back in school?

When I feel unappreciated and unloved, I ask God
how he will provide for me, because he promised to. I might
receive an unexpected card in the mail or a hug from wiry
little-boy arms. When feelings of worthlessness drove me
to *need* something big and important to do, I got something
terrifying and thrilling and way too big for me. What might
you get if you ask?

Isn't that the essence of the "Little Way" of Thérèse of
Lisieux? "I'm too little, Lord. Will you lift me?" She wanted
to be a missionary, a priest, a mother, a martyr, a Carmelite
nun. She wanted to do it *all*. And doesn't she, now, through
the millions who call upon her and follow her example?
Blessed Mother Teresa, also, wanted to do big things for
God. What do you *really* want, Dear One? Is it even possible?

To See God's Glory Revealed

Moses dreamed about doing big things with and for God.
In fact, Moses asked for the impossible.

> Moses said, "Show me your glory [Lord], I pray."
> And he said, "I will make all my goodness pass
> before you, and will proclaim before you the
> name 'The-LORD'; and I will be gracious to whom
> I will be gracious, and will show mercy on whom
> I will show mercy. But," he said, "you cannot see
> my face; for man shall not see me and live." (Ex
> 33:18–20)

What follows is, for me, one of the most tender exchanges in the scriptures. Moses made an audacious petition of God by asking him to see his glory. The word *glory* is used to denote God's presence, meaning literally "weight." God told him it was impossible. Moses asked to see the weight of God's presence, and God told him his glory is so significant as to be unbearable (1 Tm 6:16).

Because God is Spirit, the term *face* is a representation of God in familiar human form. Theologians call this *anthropomorphism*. With faultless care for the health and well-being of his friend Moses, who obviously had no idea what he had asked, the Lord would adjust himself so that he could grant the almost ridiculous request. No man could ever lay eyes on the undiluted energy of the Living Trinity, not Moses, and not you or I.

But, strangely, he was unwilling to completely deny the request, either. He would allow Moses to see *something*. Not enough to kill him, but something transcendental, something shocking and beautiful enough for Moses to face-plant before God in worship. Whatever measure of God's glory he saw, it was enough to sustain Moses through all the hardships of all the big things God wanted to accomplish through him.

Why do we, as children of God, think that after all these millennia, theologians and preachers must certainly have plumbed and explained all there is to know about God? Why do we act as if all the mysteries have already been experienced by the saints and that there is nothing left to discover for ourselves? Why are we content to read about Moses instead of dying to *be* Moses? The only thing that set Moses apart from you and me was his desire. He was so driven to know God that he asked for, received, and accomplished otherwise impossible things. Am I? What might God do in and through me if I give him everything, if I hold nothing back from him, and never surrender to anything less? Don't you long to *know*?

Perhaps we don't unleash the torrent of our true desire because we are secretly scared that God is not big enough or interested enough to satisfy such an "impossibility." Or maybe we feel blasphemous by wanting or needing anything more than he has already so graciously provided.

Oh Beloved, he is simply waiting for you to ask. There has never been a time when I have had a true, focused, desperate desire, that I was not rewarded for tenacious asking. Never. If Moses dreamed of and received what God himself considered an impossibility, then I can too. If the Lord of all creation will go out of his way to accommodate Moses's preposterous request, then what if he just might do the same for me?

Let's Review

Let's review how our patterns of desire can lead us to God:

> *My desires are meant to point me toward God.* Desires "form the passageway and ensure the connection between the life of the senses and the life of the mind" (CCC 1764).
>
> *Disordered desires are part of our human condition,* yet God can use all of my physical, emotional, intellectual, and spiritual desires to unleash my peace, wholeness, and salvation.
>
> *I must discern the truest desire under my attachment,* the one coming from my soul, in order to give it to God and find him in it.
>
> *When God gives me a desire, he can and will satisfy it,* no matter how impossible it seems, if I will tenaciously follow him to it.

An Invitation

I learned early not to hope too much for what I wanted. So when I felt that the Holy Spirit had called me to a specific work, one that fit me to a *t* and the single thing I had always wanted to be when I grew up, I went all in. Because it seemed improbable, too good to be true, I asked him if I had heard right. "And the LORD answered me: 'Write the vision; make it plain up on tablets'" (Hb 2:2). Even though the vision seemed literally impossible, I wrote down the whole call and promise as I understood it in my prayer journal. I still have it; the date of the entry is April 9, 2000.

I invested all of the energies left over from my duties to my husband and family into what I felt was this promise. After all, it was God promising me, and he cannot lie (Nm 23:19). There is no way to convey to you how badly I desired it, except to ask you what your greatest desire is and how badly you want it.

I threw myself immediately into making it happen. Only it didn't. Not for fifteen very long years. In fact, my every attempt was painfully and sometimes publicly frustrated. Dear One, I cannot tell you how excruciating and humiliating it was for me to keep trying, because every time I failed, my feelings of worthlessness, shame, and memories of repeated, hurtful reneges came galloping to the surface like an army of demons. Can you see how God used this pattern in my circumstances to draw my hurts to the surface and heal them?

Over and over I sobbed, raged, and accused God in prayer, brokenhearted and confused by the feeling that my Heavenly Father was dangling my greatest desire and my deepest fear in front of me like a carrot. Like my dad had seemed to do. Can you see how my deepest desire was meant to lead me to him?

Over and over I swore with curses that I was *done*. And sooner or later, like an idiot, I thought, I just couldn't let it go. As much as I wanted to abandon the fruitless attempts, I believed and hungered for what I thought he said I was supposed to have, so I kept risking it. Guess what?

The promise was in his arms, and he led me straight there through every painful, healing trip around the mountain. Although the promise had three parts, the book you are holding in your hands right now is the final culmination of every last line of the vision and dream I wrote in my prayer journal that morning. God is faithful, Dear One. Never, never, never give up on what your heart desires. It might just be what God desires for you. "For still the vision awaits its time; it hastens to the end—it will not lie. If it seem slow, wait for it; it will surely come, it will not delay" (Hb 2:3).

Because all growth is spiritual, I am at my best when I honor the desires of all my faculties—emotional, physical, intellectual, and spiritual. I may have desires in each area; it's all mysteriously the same unleashing. Far from being bad, what I desire most is located in the lowest ground that is my very soul, and God created my soul to strive in an upward spiral and outward to inward, toward wholeness, freedom, salvation, and peace. That's why my deepest desires can draw my attention to where God is silently working to unleash my life.

Beloved, your deepest desires are where God is already unleashing you. He wants you to join him. If you do, your desires will no longer unwittingly control your behavior, relationships, or circumstances. Instead, they will increasingly lead you straight into your Heavenly Father's arms. I and Moses and Peter are just three of the "great cloud of witnesses" who live to tell about it (Heb 12:1).

God Prompt

Remembering the Holy Spirit surrounds you with love, try to meditate on this verse, concentrating on each word in turn, until you can sense his movement in your heart. "Delight in the LORD, and he will give you the desires of your heart" (Ps 37:4). Can you trust this promise? What does it mean to "delight in the Lord"?

Attempt to discern the pattern in your deepest desires: Think back over your life. It might be that you have had different desires at different seasons of your life. What have you desired most? Did you get it? What do you desire most right now? What have you wanted longest or strongest? What have you worked hardest for?

Probe for the self-knowledge: Why do I want what I want? Disordered desires and attachments numb our hunger and capacity for God, and mask our truest needs and feelings. Fear or shame is often the reason for our attachments. Is mine a scattered or disordered desire, or do I think it's coming from God himself?

What emotion is driving my desire? Do I feel afraid, worthless? Am I in pain? Am I grasping for worth and love outwardly, or going to the only Source that can fill the gnawing emptiness in my soul?

"And my God will fully satisfy every need of yours according to his riches in glory in Christ Jesus" (Phil 4:19). Can you place yourself in this verse? What is your Heavenly Father saying to you?

Attempt to discern what you need under the desire: If I cannot answer these questions, I can ask God, and wait, and he will lead me to the answers. In his presence for as long as it takes, keep asking yourself why you want what you want until you reach the deepest, truest desire. You may want to read today's readings and see if he speaks to your heart about this desire. In the meantime, deny your disordered desire, and you will discover what your heart is truly longing for by asking these questions. Perhaps you will need to ask for grace to deny the superficial desire. Maybe you want to do so now.

This is how we can redirect scattered or disordered desires. When we redirect our scattered and disordered desires, we always find God, because what we yearn for is his touch on the neediness and weakness of our souls.

If your desire is from God: You may want to meditate on this verse. "So shall my word be that goes out from my mouth; it shall not return to me empty, but it shall accomplish that which I purpose, and succeed in the thing for which I sent it" (Is 55:11). What is the Holy Spirit saying to you?

At this time, you may also want to record your vision and desire somewhere, as best as you understand it. "Write the vision; make it plain upon tablets" (Hb 2:2).

7

Have You Never Read the Scriptures?

Unleashing the Power of God's Word

Dear One, hear Jesus ask you this question: "Have you never read the scriptures?" No doubt you have heard the Word of God proclaimed at Mass or read snippets online or in books or magazines. But have you ever taken it up to read, allowing each word to penetrate your heart until you could hear the very voice of God speaking to you as clearly as I am speaking to you now?

In this passage in the Gospel of Matthew, Jesus is challenging "religious" people who go through the motions without ever attending to the voice of the Spirit. So many Catholic women listen to the readings every week, or even every day, at Mass but never stop to consider the liberating power and desire of the Word of God in their lives, or that

God is, literally, speaking directly to them there. That so many have never experienced the mysterious encounter with the Divine Other waiting for them in the scriptures is utterly tragic to me, and I have devoted my life to helping reverse that reality.

Diving deep into scripture is the only way to become truly unleashed in our understanding of who God is and what he wants for us and from us. The sacraments are powerful sources of strength and healing, but they are only half the equation.

> The Church has always venerated the Scriptures as she venerates the Lord's Body. She never ceases to present to the faithful the bread of life, taken from *the one table of God's Word and Christ's Body.* In Sacred Scripture, the Church constantly finds her nourishment and her strength, for she welcomes it not as a human word, but as what it really is, the word of God. In the sacred books, the Father who is in heaven comes lovingly to meet his children, and talks with them. (CCC 103–4, emphasis added)

Part of the "one table" of the Lord, the Word of God offers the clear self-knowledge and understanding that are absolutely necessary to becoming truly unleashed Christians. We must let the sap of the Holy Spirit animate our religious practice so we may truly love well, and that happens particularly in the scriptures. As in all things, Mary is our strongest example. Mary hears and listens to the Word of God.

Mary, Mother of Listening

In an address in St. Peter's Square, Pope Francis once compared our ability to hear the voice of God with that of the Blessed Mother and her kinswoman Elizabeth.

What gave rise to Mary's act of going to visit her relative Elizabeth? A *word of God's* angel. "Elizabeth in her old age has also conceived a son . . ." (Lk 1:36). Mary knew how to listen to God. Be careful: it was not merely "hearing" a superficial word, but it was "listening," that consists of attention, acceptance and availability to God. It was not in the distracted way with which we sometimes face the Lord or others: we hear their words, but we do not really listen. Mary is attentive to God. She listens to God.

However Mary also listens to the events, that is, she interprets the events of her life, she is attentive to reality itself and does not stop on the surface but goes to the depths to grasp its meaning. Her kinswoman Elizabeth, who is already elderly, is expecting a child: this is the event. But Mary is attentive to the meaning. She can understand it: "with God nothing will be impossible" (Lk 1:37).

This is also true in our life: listening to God who speaks to us, and listening also to daily reality, paying attention to people, to events, because the Lord is at the door of our life and knocks in many ways, he puts signs on our path; he gives us the ability to see them. Mary is the mother of listening, of attentive listening to God and of equally attentive listening to the events of life. (emphasis added)[1]

Are you unconvinced God will speak directly to you in the scriptures? One of the questions I am asked most in my speaking and travels is: how can I know what God is saying and what he wants me to do? Isn't this question the essence of what being unleashed is? Remembering that the heart of obedience is to hear, how do I hear God? How do I seek his face?

If you are participating in the God Prompt sections at the end of each chapter, you are praying the scriptures throughout this book. Is that consoling or surprising? Even so, you may asking: *Yes, but how* exactly *can I know and hear for myself? Throughout the beautiful mess of my life, how can the scriptures teach me to cooperate most directly with the Holy Spirit to unleash my behaviors, relationships, circumstances, and desires?*

Well, let's begin with what not to do.

How *Not* to Read the Scriptures

The first time I picked up a Bible and started to read, I was frustrated by the time I got to the third chapter of Genesis. I found trying to understand it arduous and intimidating. Why were Adam and Eve suddenly ashamed after they sinned? Why *exactly*? I traced the references in my basic Bible but still didn't feel satisfied. I finally skipped it but ran immediately into another difficulty. The first book of Samuel in my Bible translation was full of the word *emerods*. I wondered what the heck an *emerod* could be and couldn't tell from the context. In an irritated pout, I told God I wasn't picking up my Bible again unless I got an answer. I'm an all-or-nothing kind of girl.

My mother was an avid reader, and the only bookshelf in our house was the one in my bedroom that ran half the length of one wall. As I was leaving the room one day, my eye caught the title on the spine of one of hundreds of books: *Bible Dictionary*. Hmmm. I checked to see if *emerod* was there: "an infected, malignant boil; a hemorrhoid." I was stunned.

Have I mentioned that I've never had a question for God that he did not somehow answer?

This question-and-answer episode catapulted me into the most exciting journey of my life: the effort to seek God's face in the scriptures. At first, I only read the Bible when I needed an answer for something. I used the Bible like a Magic 8 Ball: ask a question, let the Bible fall open where it may, and start reading.

I asked God where we should buy or build a house. The gospel included a city named Bethpage. Hey, I concluded, that's just up the road. I located land up for sale at auction and was sure God had told me we should buy land there. We were outbid, and I was shocked and mortified by how wrong I'd been. I learned not to depend solely on my own hunches when reading and discerning God's voice.

I began a broken practice of talking to God about my life, loves, observations, and problems, and reading the Bible for guidance and answers. The scriptures came alive for me: they spoke to me, had hands that took hold of me; they had feet that ran after me. I read through one book, then another, in no particular order at all.

Then I started a faithful, daily prayer time with the scriptures. I read until I felt my attention drawn to a word or sentence or passage; I would stop and write it in my prayer journal and ask God what he was trying to say to me. Then I would sit and wait and listen, and write down whatever I thought I was hearing.

Not long after I began the practice, a mentor asked me to help her teach a Bible study. I agreed, but a couple of weeks into the study, she told me she felt I was supposed to teach it myself. Oddly, I had begun to feel the same way, but figured it was a prideful thought. At that time I had never been in a single seminary class; I knew exactly nothing about anything; I was barely twenty years old. But I tried it and was hooked, and I never looked back.

I settled into a regular routine of prayer and study with the scriptures, and eventually got some formal theological training. As I learned who God was, I began writing my own

Bible study materials. The Holy Spirit seemed to be speaking at every turn as I discovered more about what God was like, his purposes, and his ways.

Getting into Scripture: Some Practical Advice

If you can't imagine yourself finding time to read or study scriptures for hours every week, please be at peace. Unless God is calling you to teaching or other formal service, you don't *need* to spend that much time reading the Bible.

Even so, in order to clearly hear God and know his will, one must immerse herself in the scriptures on a daily basis, for at least a few minutes every day. "All scripture is inspired by God and useful for teaching, for reproof, for correction, and for training in righteousness" (2 Tm 3:16). "Ignorance of the scriptures is ignorance of Christ," said St. Jerome.[2]

One way to absorb the scriptures that is both easy and enjoyable is through the ancient spiritual practice of *lectio divina* (holy reading), a practice that originated in the Church. Over time I learned not to pick texts that are pleasing to me; such selectivity is not prayer, it's self-consolation.

Instead, find a systematic schedule that works for you, and stick to it. I pray you will especially consider the daily readings from the lectionary (the Church's daily scripture schedule of readings) available online or sometimes through your parish bulletin, or by subscribing to a daily print resource such as *Magnificat* or visiting an online resource such as usccb.org or apostleshipofprayer.org).

Reading and studying scripture is more than an individual expression, because it also happens in and with the global Church. It's a community endeavor (Acts 2:42–47). Reading and studying scripture is both an individual expression of love and trust for God, as well as a communal expression of our faith.

How can our hearts be converted to the will of God if we force the Word of God to convert to a personal agenda? The simple answer is: we can't. This is especially true of scripture *study,* when we primarily want to know what the scriptures *mean.* Participating in a Catholic Bible study, six to eight weeks or so, in spring *and* fall is a good practice, but at least once a year is important. Online is fine and convenient, but with a group is better.

Please, and I am pleading, use only Catholic Bible studies and resources. Interpretation of scripture is never an individual matter: "First of all you must understand this, that no prophecy of scripture is a matter of one's own interpretation" (2 Pt 1:20). All scripture is prophecy, because it all witnesses to Christ (Rv 19:10), so we must study and read the scriptures with the Church throughout history in order to stay united to the Holy Spirit by whom they were written.

In order to read the scriptures on a daily basis with the Church, I use the Daily Office, the texts that the whole Church prays, offers, and prescribes. I adjust my practice and spirit to that, so that the Office gets me out of myself and into the flow of what the Holy Spirit is already achieving in the Church, which he has been building and nurturing for millennia.

The passages I read each day are being read all over the world, particularly the Mass readings. I am convinced the Holy Spirit saved a huge thrill for me when showing me the Office for the first time, by pointing out how my circumstances were addressed by the readings of the day, readings chosen hundreds of years before and that the whole Church prays on any given day. I can know I am in the flow of what the Holy Spirit is doing by reading the daily readings of the Church, and it's not a matter of chance at all.

Currently, my practice is to read the whole Office of Readings for the day—morning, Mass, and evening readings—altogether, in the morning after my Rosary. The Rosary and the whole Office, including a meditation with the Church Fathers and some time spent listening and contemplating, takes about one hour.

You may not have time for that, and that's fine. Simply read and pray over the gospel reading for the day. For just the gospel, I *love* the *Pray as You Go* podcast on my Laudate app or online. But before you do it, and every time you open the scriptures or hear them read out loud (at church), ask the Holy Spirit what he wants to say to you, and always expect him to speak. Do this every day, Dear One, and I promise you the Holy Spirit will be unleashed in your heart and life in wonderful ways you could never guess. But it can only happen if we, like Mary, are silent with God, pondering things in our hearts.

Sanctity's Mother Tongue

Lawrence G. Lovasik, S.V.D., missionary priest and founder of the Family Service Corps, taught that "silence is the language of God—sanctity's mother tongue."[3] The ability to be silent may be one of the most important things any of us can learn in the growth of our spiritual lives.

Is lectio divina simply reading the scriptures? If I read passage after passage, book after book of the Bible, have I really prayed if I have not listened for God's voice? And how do I know it's him I'm hearing and not my own thoughts and wishes?

There was a time when I was overly confident in my own ability to interpret God's Word for myself. But over time I learned that I simply couldn't trust my hunches; I had been wrong about them, interpreting them too subjectively or selfishly many times. On the other hand, when the words I'd read in black and white leaped off the page at me a couple of days in a row, creating a pattern, I learned to trust that it was indeed God speaking to me. I discovered I could trust and expect him to deal with me just as he dealt with his people throughout sacred time, in the same ways and patterns I read about in the scriptures. I can expect to discover some startling new insight as I chew on all I have read and studied and, like Mary, when I watch my circumstances for confirmation of what I think I am hearing. But only when I spend time in silence.

Only silence produces the quality of listening. Did you know that *silent* and *listen* are the same word with the letters in a different order? We live in a world polluted with noise. We pollute our own homes and lives with noise. How will we ever hear God speak if we cannot be silent?

As I discerned the Holy Spirit's voice and activity in my life, I asked for other helpful resources that elaborated on what I was learning. One of the most helpful subjects he led me to was human development.

God Speaks through Patterns of Human Development

While I was non-Catholic, one of the most frustrating matters in trying to live the Christian life was always the pervasive lack of direction in the spiritual life and prayer. I confess that most of my life with God has felt like blind floundering. My study of the scriptures comforts me somewhat, because all of the biblical heroes also experienced this "blindness" of faith. I am certain my own blindness is by design, because it keeps me following so closely to God that I repeatedly bump against him.

But my personality is logical and analytical. For me, lack of direction always feels a lot like stumbling into Hotel California—pervasive feelings of wrongness, being surrounded by the bizarre, and no escape available.

There are wonderful non-Catholic teachers on every subject imaginable, but the teaching on the Holy Spirit that I found in the Church was *full* of scripture, and therefore its startling beauty and depth penetrated my heart. A holy and insightful sponsor referred me to the mystics who explain the call to be unleashed by the Holy Spirit as something I am, rather than something I do. Like the Eucharist, it's something I receive rather than take. Like a tree bearing fruit, I must stay rooted in the Word—the Eucharist, the scriptures, and the Church as the mystical Body of Christ—and be open, receptive, and obedient; he does the rest.

The Collected Works of St. John of the Cross plunged me headlong into a lovely abyss of training on the process of being unleashed. I learned about the Purgative, Illuminative, and Unitive Ways, about patterns of consolation and desolation, and about the Night of the Senses and the Night of the Spirit common to those who embark on a serious pursuit of God.

To this day, I have never been so thoroughly and deeply *taught* as I was that first time reading St. John of the Cross. To my great delight, he made liberal use of the scriptures in his writings. I felt a little like a piglet in a mud puddle. I was on familiar footing, yet way in over my head in the best of ways. The Holy Spirit uses the scriptures in John of the Cross's writings to continue to speak to me more and more deeply.

St. Teresa of Avila's writings offer the same patterns within an interior castle metaphor. James Fowler's *Stages of Faith* offers more contemporary, psychological information on the upward spiral analogy. The Holy Spirit deepened and cemented the stages in my heart and mind with all I read and learned.

Imagine my relief in discovering everything I had experienced was normal and deliberate and had been mapped and communicated hundreds of years earlier, and that everyone follows the same general path. I learned that no matter how badly or how quickly I want to reach the summit in any intellectual, emotional, physical, or spiritual endeavor, until I am developmentally ready for it, it is simply impossible.

The Holy Spirit will not expect me to master trigonometry when I don't know the rudiments of algebra. He won't ask me to contemplate when I have not yet learned mediation. He will not expect me to run marathons when I am barely able to walk. Remember to expect a slow unleashing, a learning curve as you read and study the scriptures.

Don't get discouraged that you don't have verses memorized or know where certain passages are, or that you are unable to explain the intricacies of the Trinity in the scriptures or see progress immediately; you will if you stay disciplined and don't quit. These things will come. The Holy Spirit works with our natural stages of development, not despite them. Trust.

Knowing the stages of spiritual growth and prayer helped give me a sense of peace, direction, and patience. I was able to rest in my burning desire and disorientation and dryness, because I learned that burning desire and dryness and blindness are God's action and presence on my soul.

I am comforted by the knowledge that I am part of a larger whole and that my experience is common to all. I have context. I no longer judge myself or others, because I understand we are all on a similar continuum. Self-righteousness? A stage. I can pray my way out of it and on to the next stage. Holiness? I can pray and strive for that because my neighbor shows me through his life that it's possible.

On the other hand, God is neither limited nor predictable; he continues to agitate me out of comfortable habits in the most individual, surprising, personal ways. "For my thoughts are not your thoughts, nor are your ways my ways, says the LORD. For as the heavens are higher than the earth, so are my ways higher than your ways and my thoughts than your thoughts" (Is 55:8–9).

In order to understand and cooperate with what God was doing in me and in those around me, I moved insatiably from John of the Cross to Teresa of Avila to Thérèse of Lisieux. I stumbled upon James Fowler's *Stages of Faith.*

I devoured Fr. Garrigou Lagrange's *The Three Ages of the Interior Life*. In a nutshell, I learned God purifies us from the outside in, outward to inward and back out again, and that we progress in slow, careful increments in an upward spiral to him. Episodes of blindness and disorientation are necessary parts of each stage. My desires are the invisible voice of God drawing me more and more deeply into his presence, at which point I am most deeply touched and satisfied. Since then, I am reading a spiritual book of some sort all the time; I follow my interests and ask him to lead.

Ultimately, however, both the scriptures and teachings on spiritual formation issue definitively from the Church. An encounter with the Holy Spirit in the scriptures, in the writings of the Church, and at each stage of formation is an encounter with God himself in the Church.

God Speaks through the Church

Our "believe what you want to believe" culture attempts to minimize and marginalize the Church, but the Holy Spirit speaks most definitively through the teaching office of the Magisterium and the history and Tradition of the Church (which includes but is not limited to scripture).

"The pillar and foundation of truth" St. Paul describes is not my Bible, my experiences in prayer, my personal development, nor my opinions (1 Tm 3:15, NAB). This pillar and foundation is the *Church*. The Church is my measuring stick when discerning what the Holy Spirit is saying to me. The Holy Spirit is the very air the Church breathes in order to stay alive. What the Church says on an issue is what the Holy Spirit says about it. Apart from the Church I cannot fully know God's will for my life.

I have heard people say they sensed in prayer that God was telling them to do something that the scriptures or the Church, or both, say is illicit. The Bible does not speak specifically or comprehensively on every circumstance—contraception or stem-cell research, for instance—and the Church will never contradict the Bible when it's interpreted and understood properly. Certainly, then, the Holy Spirit, who gave birth to both the Church and the scriptures, would never contradict himself when speaking to an individual. I can never determine the truth of a situation by looking solely at the circumstances or my own experiences. I must know God's perspective, his wisdom, through the scriptures *and* the Church.

The Holy Spirit is not schizophrenic; he will never tell me or another individual something that contradicts the Church. I don't mean one person in the Church; I mean the Deposit of Faith as handed down to us through the last two thousand years by the Church. If I need direction or confirmation in an area where I sense God speaking, I should always search out what the scriptures and the Church have said on the subject.

I can obey the Church, and therefore obey God, but if I disobey the Church, I have disobeyed God himself. "Let every person be subject to the governing authorities; for there is no authority except from God, and those that exist have been instituted by God. Therefore whoever resists authorities resists what God has appointed, and those who resist will incur judgment" (Rom 13:1–2).

Within the Church, I can hear God speak through the scriptures. The sacraments, as catalysts and facilitators of spiritual and human development, also assist the unleashing of the Holy Spirit in my life, particularly through the Eucharist and counsel of Confession. I function in relationship to the Church, so I can hear God speak in, with, and through the Church. In the Church, I have everything I need to experience God unleashing my behaviors, relationships, circumstances, and desires.

Let's Review

Let's review how God's Word is unleashed in our lives:

> *The Word of God is a person, not a book.* He is present
> in the Eucharist, the Church as the mystical Body
> of Christ, *and* the scriptures.
>
> *The Holy Spirit is always inviting me to a fuller*
> *relationship* with his Word.
>
> *I can make Mary my model of a listener and*
> *meditate on the ways she listened* to the Word of God,
> particularly through the mysteries of the Rosary,
> which are based completely on scripture.
>
> *The Holy Spirit is always speaking and working*
> *in the scriptures* and wants me to know him, his
> purposes, ways, and will, so I can cooperate with
> him.
>
> *The Holy Spirit speaks* generally *through the*
> *common, natural human stages of development.*
>
> *The Holy Spirit speaks more* specifically
> *through the Church.*
>
> *When my development, the scriptures, and the*
> *Church all line up,* I can be reasonably certain I am
> hearing from God. If any one of them doesn't,
> I probably am not. I should wait and search for
> clarification if I am not sure.
>
> *Unleashed is who I am in God, more than some-*
> *thing I do.* I learn to hear God by obeying him and
> cooperating with him where he is working.

An Invitation

Our church was making a mission trip to Poland. The whole
team had been assembled, but the mission coordinator came
to my husband and I and said he felt the Holy Spirit had
told him we were supposed to go. I was somewhat offended;

why would the Holy Spirit not tell us first? Besides, what could we possibly contribute?

I asked everyone at church, "Do you think this is really God speaking? Here's what I think. What do you think?" I depended on other people's opinions rather than on the relationship I had with God. I looked for a burning bush. At some point I finally said, "Lord, I really want to know your will. Stop me if I am wrong, and bless me if I am right." Still, everything in my circumstances and prayer conflicted to the point that I was totally confused.

Yet this, too, confused me, for I knew that "God is not a God of confusion but of peace" (1 Cor 14:33). Did God want us to go on the mission trip or not?

Discernment on the issue took months, because the Holy Spirit was teaching me how to hear. I learned if I want to know the will and voice of God, I must give him the time and effort to nurture my relationship with him in the scriptures. I learned he is speaking and will speak there within the context of the Church. It is I who am too busy and distracted by noise to hear.

Finally I said, "I'm going to God to clarify what I am fairly sure he is saying to me. Then I am going to wait to see if and how he confirms it." As I waited and watched, I began to experience a clear, personal way that God was making his ways known to me. He revealed himself to me through prayer with the scriptures, circumstances, relationships, and the desire of my heart. "Go into all the world and preach the gospel to the whole creation" (Mk 16:15). We went to Poland, and it was one of the most powerful experiences of my life.

Dear One, the Holy Spirit is unleashed, and will unleash you, through the Word. If you have never heard him speak there, I pray you will begin a regular prayer practice in the scriptures today.

He is already at work. He wants you to join him. If you do, you will see for yourself all the wild, personal, wonderful patterns that comprise what God is doing in your life, because the Holy Spirit is waiting with bated breath to be unleashed, to show you with great certainty how he wants to unleash your behavior, relationships, circumstances, and desires.

God Prompt

Do you currently have a daily scripture habit? If you are unsure how to begin, here are some principles that have helped me grow in my own understanding of God's Word. You may need or want to adapt them for your own use, according to what God is asking of you. I merely share these as a starting point for you to consider.

First thing in the morning, go to your prayer space: From their first years, I have always instructed my children that my prayer time is off limits to them. Luckily, I already had the habit for a couple of years before they were born. I guarded my prayer time partly to model and teach them the importance of having their own, but also, I confess, because I would be crazy without it. I think they *know* this somehow. I enjoy an uninterrupted hour now, because I started with ten minutes when they were young and worked my way up as we all grew able. I often had to make arrangements for breakfast and school clothes and lunch boxes ahead of time. Sometimes I had to get up *very* early so they were not awake, and therefore I often slept through most of it. You will have to guard this time if you're going to have it at all, and God will bless your effort if you stay with it.

Today I go to the porch of my farmhouse in the spring, summer, and fall, and in front of the fire in the winter. Praying first helps me to prioritize the rest of my day. Although I am not a morning person (understated), the scriptures are full of the exhortation to connect with God first thing.

"O LORD, in the morning you hear my voice; in the morning I prepare a sacrifice for you, and watch" (Ps 5:3).

"Satisfy us in the morning with your steadfast love, so that we may rejoice and be glad all our days" (Ps 90:14).

"His mercies are new every morning" (Lam 3:22–23).

I begin with the Rosary. Then I write all my current requests, issues, questions, concerns, and problems in my prayer journal and talk to God about them. In the past, I have actually ripped holes in the paper with my pen, I was so angry, and there are tear stains on several pages of all my journals to this day. In my journal, I am brutally honest with God because I know he can and wants to handle the whole truth. Writing things down helps me clear my mind, and get ready to hear directly from God in his Word.

Once you have made yourself ready to hear from God, read the readings of the Church for the day with an openness to God's movement and voice: As a Secular Carmelite, I am supposed to read the morning, evening, and night prayers at those hours, but my duties and station in life do not allow for that, so I am allowed to read them all at once. As I do, I record any thoughts that surface and any responses or promptings from God in my journal. I research words or meanings I have questions about in a Bible dictionary, commentaries, the *Catechism of the Catholic Church,* or other Catholic references.

As you read and study, remember that a single verse can have several "senses" of meaning (see CCC 115–19). As you discern what God is saying to you, look for the *literal* meaning, that is, what the original author of the passage meant to say about the people and events of that time. But also pay careful attention to how it might apply to your own life, here and now. Be sure to write down your impressions, then watch to see where he is working and how what you

learned can affect the rest of your day. Remember to anticipate those pop quizzes.

*Take time to ponder what you have already learned, to help
you discern self-knowledge God might be communicating through
patterns in your life:* After a couple of weeks, look back at
your notes and review your impressions. What does the
Holy Spirit seem to be saying to you through your reading,
writings, and circumstances? When the Holy Spirit speaks to
you, he is speaking about you. What adjustments is the Holy
Spirit asking you to make in your behavior, relationships,
circumstances, and desires this week?

What if nothing seems to be happening? The *Catechism of
the Catholic Church* has a wonderful quotation about this,
based on the Epistle of James.

> "You ask and do not receive, because you ask
> wrongly, to spend it on your passions" (Jas 4:3).
> We ask with a divided heart, we are "adulterers"
> (Jas 4:4); God cannot answer us, for he desires our
> well-being, our life. "Or do you suppose that it
> is in vain that the scripture says, 'He yearns jeal-
> ously over the spirit which he has made to dwell
> in us'?" (Jas 4:5). That our God is "jealous" for us
> is a sign of how true his love is. If we enter into
> the desire of his Spirit, we shall be heard.
>   "Do not be troubled if you do not imme-
> diately receive from God what you ask him; for
> he desires to do something even greater for you,
> while you cling to him in prayer."[4] "God wills that
> our desire should be exercised in prayer, that we
> may be able to receive what he is prepared to
> give."[5] (CCC 2737)

The ultimate principle is: he always answers. If you don't
get a clear "yes" or "no," the answer is "wait."

What if you need to hear from God now, *such as when making an important decision?* Waiting can be hard, and yet if I do

not have clear instruction from God in a matter, I must pray and wait. I learn patience. God's timing is always right and best. Until I get a clear word from him, I obey the last clear word I received. He may withhold instructions to cause me to seek him more earnestly. I do not attempt to skip over being with God in order to get to the doing. My relationship with God is more important than what I can do for him.

The scriptures tell us that God's Word "is a lamp to my feet and a light to my path" (Ps 119:105). How does the Holy Spirit want you to incorporate more scripture into your life, so that your pathway will shine with the light of his guidance? What small step can you make today to begin doing this?

Let's take a moment to ask the assistance of Jesus' mother, a true woman of listening, who understands how hard it can be to wait on God for his perfect time.

> Mary, woman of listening, open our ears; grant us to know how to listen to the word of your Son Jesus among the thousands of words of this world; grant that we may listen to the reality in which we live, to every person we encounter, especially those who are poor, in need, in hardship.
>
> Mary, woman of decision, illuminate our minds and our hearts, so that we may obey, unhesitatingly, the word of your Son Jesus; give us the courage to decide, not to let ourselves be dragged along, letting others direct our lives.
>
> Mary, woman of action, obtain that our hands and feet move with haste toward others, to bring them the charity and love of your Son Jesus, to bring the light of the Gospel to the world, as you did. Amen.[6]

$\mathcal{D}$o You Believe This?

John 11:26

Real-Life Miracles Ahead
A Final Lesson in Faith Unleashed

From the first burst of God's Word that created every photon, atom and molecule of matter, and millisecond of time, to the Incarnation that brought his Word to bear on our darkness of soul, the Holy Spirit has been at work through Jesus, miraculously creating, ordering, illuminating, generating—*unleashing*.

Hidden no more, from the opening lines of the gospels Jesus walks into our history, our world, and our lives as no other ever has. Jesus brings God to us. Jesus is among us.

In this question from the Gospel of John, Jesus is in the cemetery with us. Death has claimed someone he loves, too, and through his grief, he takes the opportunity to teach us

the most important lesson we can learn this shadowy side
of eternity.

But Jesus doesn't teach like the prophets or the Phari-
sees or any other teacher we've ever known. Every utterance
of this man is power. Not a syllable is lost. Nothing returns
empty. Every vowel and consonant pushes forward with
purpose and intent. It accomplishes what is spoken. And
Jesus doesn't hold his words over our heads like a mallet.
He simply holds it all up to the light, like a prism, so that
an entire spectrum of color can wash over an ashen human
race. "Do you believe this?"

The Now

When is the Holy Spirit unleashed in my life? How long
does it take? Theologians tell us that God exists in an eternal moment. The scriptures say that a day with God is as a
thousand years (2 Pt 3:8). Are you ever discouraged by how
slowly God seems to work? Do you find yourself living in
the past, or always hoping for a future time when things will
be better? Perhaps in those moments, we're focusing on the
wrong time, completely.

That's what Jesus taught Mary and Martha in chapter
eleven of the Gospel of John. Lazarus was sick, so they sent
for Jesus. What else would they do? After the scriptures
carefully point out the depth of his love for this little family,
Jesus does what seems to be the rudest thing. He ignores
them for two days. He stays where he is without sending
word, and only finally reaches their house after Lazarus has
been dead for four days. On purpose.

Martha meets him on the road with what I know is a
reluctant but desperate accusation, yet with vestiges of faith
clinging to it: "Lord, if you had been here, my brother would
not have died. But even now I know that whatever you ask

of God, God will give you" (Jn 11:21–22). Intertwined with suspicion, she lays out the irresistible gauntlet: faith.

I bet it was painful for him to hold back what he was about to do, what he was going to show her, what he was about to work. I bet the power of his mercy was pressed against the veil of his flesh, straining for release. Yet slowly, deliberately, he takes the time to lead her out of the shadows of death and into a breathtaking reality. Jesus knows that Martha is living in the past, and she must move beyond that, allow him to heal it, or she cannot move forward. We know this because he directs her to the present, laying the sentence softly before her: "Your brother will rise again" (Jn 11:23)

"I know that he will rise again in the resurrection at the last day," she says (Jn 11:24). Faithfully willing to be led out of the past, she nevertheless switches to a contemplation of the future, when it will finally be okay. She understands the greatness of resurrection, but not for herself. Not now. Could she have guessed the purpose he had in mind for her from the foundation of the world, the purpose about to break in on all of them in a handful of moments more?

He painstakingly redirects her attention again, for her purpose is not in the future. To experience what is about to happen, imminent glory, she must be where Jesus is, in the eternal now: "I am [right now] the resurrection and the life. He who believes in me, though he die, yet he shall live, and whoever lives and believes in me will never die. Do you believe this?" (Jn 11:25–26).

Do *you* believe this? Something of you died, back there in your past, and you wrapped it carefully in preservatives and grave clothes and hid it away behind a stone in your heart. *If Jesus had been there it would not have happened*, you think. I know it hurts, but he let it, Dear One. He let it happen for this moment. He yearns to show you what he can do with it. Do you believe he can resurrect it so that it will never die again? Do you believe this, Most Precious One?

Listen to me. Do not look to the future, when things will be better. It cannot be better if it is still dead. It will never be better, then, unless you answer him now. He is "I Am." The resurrection is now. The life is right now. If you believe, with Martha and Mary, that he is the Christ, the Son of God come into the world for such, you must remove the stone, open the grave, and allow him to call it forward in all its deadly odor and trappings. You cannot be unleashed otherwise.

A grueling lesson, surely, but I have learned to wait silently in the midst of my deepest pain, because I have seen with Martha and Mary that when the whole thing shakes out, the ignorance, childishness, and lack of faith with which I accuse him to his face will ultimately shame me for its pride when divine love is revealed under the trappings of requiem. He only does wondrous things, the psalmist says. "Do you believe this?"

What I know now is that whatever suffering we go through, however late, dark, silent, and absent he seems, there is intention in what he allows, and it is necessary for a shrouded end. If we can brave the pain, we will see him weeping there beside us, waiting to unleash something miraculous and beautiful at our "yes." When the "Come forth" has been uttered from the lips of I Am, we must cling in faith till the grave is fully emptied, and be patient with the removal of the wrappings and the unsteady coming forth of life. If we can do this, we will surely see something unheard of and unspeakable. This is my prayer for you.

Whenever I am facing what looks like a hopeless situation or circumstance, I remember the angel Gabriel telling Mary, "For nothing will be impossible with God" (Lk 1:37). I pray, and then hide and wait to see what spectacular thing he's going to do. I am making room for the unleashing of God that produces miracles in my heart and life. When the Holy Spirit is unleashed, the dead are raised, prayers are always answered, and dry bones live. Jesus asks us, "Do you believe this?" Even when the awful 4:00 a.m. phone call crashes into your life?

The Answer to Prayer Is Always "Fish"

She was almost old enough to be my mother, the holiest woman I knew, and she sat in the front row of my Bible study class. We could not have been more different. She was in her forties, I in my twenties; she was quiet and serene, I an alligator mouth; she was deliberate, I impulsive; everything she ate flew to her hips, and I was tall, and well, I have always been too thin, everyone says, but Georgia never made uncomplimentary comments. The solitary thing we shared was a total abandonment to God.

Georgia began sending me cards in the mail, cards of encouragement and friendship, a very humbling experience for a young Bible teacher, because although I was immature and full of myself, I couldn't for the life of me see why she wanted to be my friend. And to be honest it was a little disconcerting that I struggled, at first, to feel the connection she so freely acknowledged. So when she called me one morning at four a.m. to tell me her only child, her twenty-year-old son Kevyn, had been killed in a car crash after having fallen asleep on the way home from a Christian concert, I fell to my knees in fear.

In a job, a marriage, and a life that lacked loads of satisfaction or fulfillment at the time, Kevyn was her only worldly treasure. Every morning of his elementary and high school life, she got up at half past four, her only free time, to get in an hour of lectio divina before she cooked him a full breakfast. Then they would head off to whatever school he attended, where she always worked as a teacher's aide to stay involved.

Obedient and sweet, with a deep respect for his mother, Kevyn had begun making his first forays into a local college and girlfriends, and Georgia had suddenly become gripped with flashes of fear for his safety that drove her to her knees, to the Psalms, and to fast for his protection. It was with this intimate knowledge that I received her terrified words. I asked God that fateful morning, "How could you do this to her?" I will never forget his answer, so definitive, so still, so absolute.

Totally ignorant, having no experience with death, and still in the "I don't go to funerals" stage of youth—though she never asked me to come be with her—I was afraid to go. What could I possibly say or do to help in any fathomable way? My husband, with a strong gift of mercy, simply said I should, and since I had no idea at all what to do, I went, although with great trepidation and reluctance for my powerlessness.

I rarely said anything at all as she plodded the gauntlet of planning a wake and funeral. When I felt most inept and utterly helpless, God's words to me boiled in my mind and heart, both full of accusation: "What father among you would hand his son a snake when he asks for a fish?" (Lk 11:11, NAB).

Although I suspected I was simply immature and obviously missing something, I failed to see how the death of this precious woman's only child could be anything other than a striking viper spewing the nastiest, deadliest poison. We had been praying and fasting for Kevyn's protection for months, and now he lay unrecognizably burned in a casket, her twenty-year-old baby's face closed to her for all time. A mother's terror.

I watched her go through everything in peace, even joy at times, between the deepest tears of human sorrow and complete loss—the valley of the shadow of death and grief. I, however, felt offended by what seemed to be God's meanness. She had always credited me with inspiring her to follow God, and look where it had led her? And yet, ten years later, Georgia stunned me by saying all was well, that

God had actually answered her prayers, that she could see *why*, and that what he had done was not only right, but good. I was almost appalled, but so thankful for both our sakes.

Years later, when Georgia and I had long become separated by circumstances, and I had been homeschooling my nine-year-old son for three years, we began having difficulties in math and in some areas of responsibility. A passionate teacher, I know that when someone is not getting it it's usually because I'm not communicating it well, but our daily struggles were still irritating, and our relationship had become defined by them.

I spent painful time soul searching, I had my son's learning style evaluated, and we began to make significant progress in math, but my critical spirit had isolated us from one another somewhat, and I could not recover my mother's footing with him. I knew the problem lay with me but could not find it or fix it, and all I could do was pray desperately for help.

Not even a week later, on Christmas morning, my son had a devastating accident, requiring emergency transfer to a larger city, ICU, and major reconstructive surgery that left him flat on his back for four long, arduous months. Armed with Georgia's experience and my pitiful fish, I fought back the debilitating fear and pain of our family and clung to the absolute knowledge that this was my answer, and it was the best I could receive.

After many months of painful wailing and gnashing of teeth by everyone in our family, my son hobbled to the bathroom on his walker, and from the kitchen I heard him say, "Mom, I'm kinda glad I had my accident."

My heart almost stopped. God had mercifully shown me the beautiful product of our family's recent suffering, but I dared not breathe out loud into everyone's barely healed wounds what sounded cold and callous even in my own ears.

Without breathing, I squeaked out, "What do you mean?" in as normal a voice as I could gather, and his little boy's voice, so sweet and innocent, uttered, "Because God brought us closer together."

Remembering those precious words profoundly humbles me, because it was through his sacrifice I learned that when we pray for a fish, Dear One, what we get is a fish, no matter how much it looks like a snake.

A fish? Sure. Let's look again at that passage from Luke that God whispered to my heart as I tried to comfort my grieving friend:

> What father among you would hand his son a snake when he asks for a fish? Or hand him a scorpion when he asks for an egg? If you then, who are wicked, know how to give good gifts to your children, how much more will the Father in heaven give the holy Spirit to those who ask him? (Lk 11:11–13, NAB)

But what if it's too late to ask?

Dry Bones Live

> The hand of the LORD was upon me, and he brought me out by the Spirit of the LORD, and set me down in the midst of the valley; it was full of bones. And he led me round among them; and behold, there were very many upon the valley; and lo, they were very dry. (Ez 37:1–2)

At some point, don't we all have cause to survey our lives, to confront the dead bodies strewn over the landscape of our personal histories? Whatever your tragedy, wreckage, turmoil, and issues, I hope you have been able to take a hard look at them with me, one by one, face them for what they are and whatever state they're in, and ask your Heavenly Father for a fish.

My relationship with my father and other men I respected was like the Valley of Dry Bones, strewn with dead and dried up skeletons: confrontations, fears, accusations, judgments, injuries, and damage. My relationships were nothing but skeletal remains, but the issues were no longer about "those people"; they were about me.

Even after my dad extended the olive branch and sent me that pink birthday card, I realized I had no idea how to relate to him—only that I should try, somehow. "Honor your father and mother (this is the first commandment with a promise), that it may be well with you and that you may live long on the earth" (Eph 6:2–3). Not only was my relationship with my dad difficult, but I continued to struggle in my relationship with God, my husband, and employers too. I seemed to encounter triggers with men in several areas. I suffered my weakness and neediness over and over when God pulled at the roots of my pain, and I wondered if I would ever be free of anger and fear and insecurity. Could I ever have warm, functional relationships with my dad, husband, employers, sons?

The bones in the valley of the Ezekiel passage depict death, many deaths. According to Jewish custom, it was an indignity and indecency for bodies to remain unburied, especially until the bones were exposed. No one cared enough to even bury the bodies in the Valley of Dry Bones.

To me the bones strewn over the valley are a metaphor for all the dead and decomposed relationships and circumstances scattered throughout my life. How could they be buried when I could barely look at them? What do the dry bones symbolize for you? Can you name them? "And he said to me, 'Son of man, can these bones live?' And I answered, 'O Lord GOD, thou knowest'" (Ez 37:3). What's the answer to such a question? Can your dry bones live? Isn't the answer obviously no?

Although I had to consciously do so many times, when I was able to forgive my father and truly accept him for who he is, faults and all, I experienced something miraculous that was not unlike Lazarus, Mary, Martha, Georgia, and Ezekiel's experiences of death:

> He said to me, "Prophesy to these bones, and say to them, O dry bones, hear the word of the Lord." So I prophesied as I was commanded; and as I prophesied, there was a noise, and behold, a rattling; and the bones came together, bone to its bone. And as I looked, there were sinews on them, and flesh had come upon them, and skin had covered them; but there was no breath in them." (Ez 37:4, 7–8)

What will happen if you allow the Holy Spirit continuous access, a continuous unleashing, of his slow, gentle word over your Valley of Dry Bones? As I continued, daily, to unleash the Holy Spirit through the scriptures into and onto every aspect of my dried up, skeletal life, my heart changed. My dry bones came together. I discovered new sinew and flesh and skin on all that had littered the valley of death in my soul. I forgave God for all my pain and fell in love with him. I reestablished a connection with my dad. Relationships improved, circumstances changed; I could practice virtue more consistently; I was able to trust God through my fears; I was able to treat people with love. And still, for a long time none of it seemed spiritually *alive*. I still walked around with that tightness settled on my chest like an x–ray apron, always waiting for the blast that would finally irradiate me.

> Then he said to me, "Prophesy to the breath, prophesy, son of man, and say to the breath, Thus says the Lord GOD: Come from the four winds, O breath, and breathe upon these slain, that they

may live." So I prophesied as he commanded me,
and the breath came into them, and they lived,
and stood upon their feet, an exceedingly great
host. (Ez 37:9–10)

Breath here is "spirit." The Holy Spirit, through the word,
is *unleashed*.

Let's Review

Before we draw our journey together to a close, let's do a
wrap-up survey of how we can unleash the Holy Spirit into
our lives, so our habits, relationships, circumstances, and
desires can be unleashed.

> *The Holy Spirit wants to be unleashed into all of the
> areas of my life.* I should ask him to begin work-
> ing, and be specific, complete, and truthful about
> where I want and need his unleashing, holding
> nothing back. When I do, he immediately gets
> busy. I should be prepared for my issues to get
> worse, sometimes far worse, before they get bet-
> ter; I will not give up simply because it's hard.
>
> *Although his power is matchless, he works
> slowly and gently,* with (not despite) my person-
> ality and temperament, current circumstances
> and relationships, and spiritual development.
> His pattern is outward to inward and upward
> spiral. I will encounter desert episodes, because I
> am unleashed most effectively from my predom-
> inant fault in the desert.
>
> *The patterns in my circumstances and rela-
> tionships show me where the Holy Spirit is working*
> and wants me to cooperate with him. When the
> Holy Spirit speaks to me, he is speaking about
> me. Circumstances and relationships often
> grow more difficult the longer it takes for them

to get my attention and the more I succumb to comfort-seeking behaviors. My worst pattern of emotional eruptions reveals my predominant fault, which is the weakest and most bound-up point of my soul.

Suffering is not punishment from God. Because Jesus' sacrifice changed and redeemed suffering, my suffering can and will purify my heart and life if I will cooperate with it. When I experience something several times, I should pay attention, because the Holy Spirit may be attempting to get my attention.

My deepest, truest desires will always lead me to God, who gave them to me in order to fulfill them. The fulfillment of my deepest desires may take a decade or more, but it will surely come to pass if I work steadily and patiently with the Holy Spirit.

To hear God speak to me personally and consistently, I must listen to Church teachings, participate in regular Bible study, and have a daily reading and silent listening practice in the scriptures.

If I believe God will move and work miraculously in my life, he most certainly will, as I choose to open myself to receive all that the Holy Spirit wants to give me and act on my belief by cooperating with him.

An Invitation

Your unleashing has already begun. Take comfort in knowing I am offering ongoing prayers and sacrifices specifically for you. The Holy Spirit is already at work in your habits, relationships, circumstances, and desires. He will lead you in more specific ways if you are listening for his voice of power and unleashing in the scriptures every day. If you have not already, will you begin, today, reading at least the gospel readings every day, asking God to speak and listening silently for his voice?

God Prompt

Which of the three stories from this chapter speaks to you the most? Why?

Does the history of your life feel more like a Valley of Dry Bones, littered and strewn with corpses, or like a grave containing a single, horrifying incident or occurrence that is sealed behind a stone?

Can you talk to God about that now? Are you willing to bring his word to bear on all of it? What specific action in the scriptures will you take in order for this to happen?

I have a feeling you know exactly what you want to pray now. Whatever you feel in your heart, offer it to Jesus, Dear One. Cling to your "fish," do whatever he tells you, and wait for the resurrection, because miracles always happen when the Holy Spirit is unleashed.

"You have not only a glorious history to remember and recount, but also a great history still to be accomplished. Look to the future, where the Spirit is sending you in order to do even greater things" (St. John Paul II, *Vita Consecrata*).

For Group Reading and Study

Have you ever noticed that people live for themselves what they learn for themselves? That's why at the end of almost every chapter of *Unleashed* there are three special sections: *Let's Review*, where we summarize the main points of the chapter; *An Invitation*, where the Holy Spirit invites us to go deeper; and a *God Prompt* containing personal scripture exercises that help connect us directly to God through contemplation and prayer.

You may want to meet with a circle of friends for sharing and fellowship while working through each chapter and section yourself. You may also want to watch the *Unleashed* DVD series that complements the book together as a group. After all, aren't sharing and fellowship rich sources of fun, continued learning, community, and faith support? Following your introductory week, participants might meet for eight weeks of forty-five-minute to one-hour group discussion sessions that provide a community in which to share insights and applications gleaned throughout the week.

Since the personal application sections at the end of each chapter may be too intimate and private for some to feel comfortable sharing, I provided this collection of questions for those who want to meet together with others. If you are interested in the possibility of forming a group but would feel more comfortable with extra guidance, see the Group Facilitator's Guide directly following these group questions.

Group Questions

Introduction

As you study the cover and title of the book, what are your impressions? Do you think everyone needs to be "unleashed" by the Holy Spirit in some way? Was Mary, Jesus' mother, unleashed?

After you have read through the foreword and introduction together, either silently or aloud as a group, discuss: What do you hope to take away from this study? What do you want the Holy Spirit to do in your life?

If you brought a Bible, thumb through it for a moment or two. Thinking back over your life, try to describe your relationship with the scriptures in one word.

What, if anything, bothers you the most about the Bible? What about it makes you most uncomfortable? How do you hope or anticipate your relationship with the scriptures to change as you work through this book?

Pray a closing Our Father, Hail Mary, and Glory Be together.

1. What Do You Wish?

- Read through the *Let's Review* section together. What is the most significant point in this review for you?
- If you feel comfortable sharing, what is your answer to Jesus' question, "What do you wish?"
- When you think about sacred and secular history, do they seem like two separate collections of stories? If so, to which part do you feel most strongly connected, and why?

- Have you ever considered the scriptures as God's speaking directly to you? How does looking at the Bible that way make you feel?
- As a group, turn to Hebrews 13:2.[1] Before you read and discuss this verse, have at least two members of your group read the verse from a different translation, and compare the versions of this verse in your group. Based on what you have read, how does "hospitality" relate to this passage?
- What was the sentence, scripture, or idea that was most significant to you in this chapter? What stood out the most? Read through *An Invitation* together. What do you look forward to the most as you consider what's to come in this book?
- Pray a closing Our Father, Hail Mary, and Glory Be together.

2. Who Touched Me?

- Have you ever tried to read the Bible straight through? Did you finish? Explain.
- Read through the *Let's Review* section together. What is the most significant point in this review for you? Explain. If you marked or noted an especially meaningful sentence or idea in your book as you read this chapter, you may want to share your insight or thoughts now.
- What, if anything, did you learn or relearn about how God works in our lives through this chapter?
- If you like, share your driest or darkest desert time. What, if anything, did you discover through those experiences?
- What, if anything, did you sense God was saying to you through the scripture exercise in the *God Prompt*?
- Pray a closing Our Father, Hail Mary, and Glory Be or spontaneous prayer together.

3. Has No One Condemned You?

- Read through *Let's Review* together. Which point is most significant for you? If you marked a sentence, verse, or idea in this chapter, you may want to share it now.
- As you read the story about the woman caught in adultery, with which character do you most identify, and why?
- Has your understanding or awareness of sin changed from reading this chapter?
- As a group, look up Wisdom 11:16 and Jeremiah 2:19. Compare the verse in several translations, and discuss how these verses apply to your understanding of sin, judgment, or punishment.
- Some view suffering as punishment from God. What do you think is the purpose of suffering? Does it have a purpose?
- As you review your life, can you share a time when S + P = B applied to your circumstances?
- Pray the Come, Holy Spirit prayer at the end of the chapter together.

4. Why Do You See the Speck in Your Neighbor's Eye, but Do Not Notice the Log in Your Own Eye?

- Read through *Let's Review* together. Which of these points is most significant to you? If you marked a sentence, verse, or idea in this chapter, you may want to share it now.
- Why do you think the saints insist that self-knowledge is the foundation for spiritual growth?
- How is growth in self-knowledge related to growth in relationships?
- As a group, look up 1 Corinthians 6:3. Compare the translation of different versions, and discuss: Is judgment different from evaluation? Explain.

- One of the biblical examples of relationship difficulties offered in this chapter is that of Cain and Abel. Can you think of other examples from the scriptures that illustrate the points of this chapter?
- Has your understanding of neediness and weakness changed through this chapter? If so, how?
- Pray a closing Our Father, Hail Mary, and Glory Be or spontaneous prayer together.

5. Why Do You Call Me "Lord, Lord" but Not Do What I Command?

- Turn to *Let's Review,* and read through it together. What stands out most in these points for you? If you marked a sentence, verse, or idea in this chapter, you may want to share it now.
- Looking back on your life, what has been your typical reaction to pain, negative circumstances, and suffering? Have you ever experienced something tragic, painful, or negative that turned out to be fortuitous or to have a silver lining?
- As a group, read and discuss Hebrews 5:7–8. How does it make you feel to know Jesus learned to hear God through the things he suffered?
- Read and exchange thoughts on 1 Peter 4:1–2. What does this passage mean to you?
- Have you experienced any pop quizzes throughout your reading of *Unleashed*?
- Pray a closing Our Father, Hail Mary, and Glory Be or spontaneous prayer together.

6. Do You Love Me?

- Read through and exchange thoughts on *Let's Review* together. If you marked a sentence, verse, or idea in this chapter, you may want to share it now.
- Do you have a Big Dream you'd like to share? What might this dream require of you? Have you given up on receiving its fulfillment? Why or why not?

- As a group, read and discuss Philippians 4:19. What scares you most about your deepest desires? Are there any superficial desires that are "masking" deeper, more important desires? How does this verse pertain to that?
- As a group, read and discuss Psalm 37:3–4. How do you feel about the possibility that God might want your dream for you as much or more than you want it for yourself?
- Pray a closing Our Father, Hail Mary, and Glory Be or spontaneous prayer together.

7. Have You Never Read the Scriptures?

- Read through and discuss *Let's Review* together as a group. Which point is most significant to you? If you marked a sentence, verse, or idea in this chapter, you may want to share it now.
- Have you begun a regular practice in the scriptures, either this week or previously? What's the most exciting or personally meaningful thing you have ever learned through the scriptures? What has been your worst or most frustrating experience in the scriptures?
- How might meditating on the Joyful Mysteries of the Rosary and the life of Mary change as you contemplate her as the Mother of Listening?
- When God attempts to create something new in our lives or move us from one stage of spiritual development to another, the first thing he does is agitate us out of our comfort zones. Throughout our chapters of reading you may have encountered new information that excited, challenged, annoyed, or disturbed you. Did that happen to you?
- Pray a closing Our Father, Hail Mary, and Glory Be or spontaneous prayer together.

8. Do You Believe This?

- As a group, spend some time talking about each point of the *Let's Review* section. If you marked a sentence, verse, or idea in this chapter, you may want to share it now.
- Throughout your reading and study, have you identified any patterns in your habits, relationships, or circumstances through which the Holy Spirit is at work? Would you like to share your predominant fault?
- Have you been completely transparent with God about where you want and need his unleashing? (If it is difficult to share in a group setting, that's okay. Consider going to Confession or making an appointment with your pastor to discuss this instead.)
- Do you ever grow impatient with how slowly he seems to work? Can you see your own progression through the inward to outward and upward spiral pattern?
- How can you get more scripture in your spiritual diet? Has your view of the Bible changed at all throughout this book?
- If you had to identify the most important thing the Holy Spirit wants you to take away from this book, what would that be? Is it different from what you hoped for from him in the beginning of our journey together?
- Which of the stories from this chapter speaks to you the most? Why?
- Spend a few moments in silent prayer. Thank God for all he has done and will continue to do. Then pray this prayer or some other together:

> Heavenly Father,
> I believe; help my unbelief.
> I am not worthy to receive you, but only say the
>   word and I shall be healed.

I open the doors of my soul wide to you. Unleash
    me from all that prevents me from having
    a perfect union with you.
Help me to listen to your Holy Spirit, just as your
    Son, Jesus, listened to his mother, Mary.
    Help me to trust you like he trusted her.
Into your hands, I commend my spirit, and the
    spirits of all those I love. Never cease
    unleashing me, so that I can help unleash
    others, all the days of my life. Amen.

Group Facilitator's Guide

Whether this is the first time you have ever led a group study, or if it is just the first time you're reading *Unleashed*, here are a few suggestions to get you started.

What is the job of a facilitator? The beauty of this format is that the only requirement needed to facilitate an *Unleashed* group study is a willingness to facilitate and a desire to help others draw closer to God through the scriptures. The most important element in the success of your group will be your own commitment to Christ and the weekly reading and exercises.

Depending on the needs of your group, many facilitators also provide some kind of administrative leadership for the group by

- scheduling, promoting, and coordinating the *Unleashed* group study;
- ordering and distributing the books;
- greeting, encouraging, and communicating with participants;
- guiding (and sometimes charitably limiting) group discussion;
- facilitating prayer intentions and group prayers;
- arranging for simple refreshments or other forms of hospitality; and
- encouraging participants to complete the reading and exercises before each class.

How to lead the group study. After receiving the books, take a few minutes to look through your copy to familiarize yourself with the book's format before distributing and introducing copies to the other participants. Each participant should have his or her own copy of *Unleashed* as well as a Catholic study Bible such as the *Revised Standard Version: Catholic Edition* or the *New American Bible*.

The book's eight chapters divide easily into eight weeks of group discussion lasting forty-five minutes to one hour. You may also wish to add an introductory week at the beginning of the study for administering information on restroom and other facilities, introductions, passing out books, pointing out the special features of each chapter, and discussing the introductory questions provided in this guide. The introductory questions can be answered without having read a word of the book and will help launch each participant into her individual reading. The introductory week is the perfect time for you as the facilitator to recommend that each member bring her Bible to every meeting, since you will be using them a lot.

Each group meeting might look like this: begin with prayer; welcome participants; make introductions, if needed; answer the questions for the chapter; pray a closing prayer; receive prayer requests and intentions.

You may get to all the questions provided for the chapter each week, and you may not. Some fellowship groups like to offer food and beverages; some don't. Some groups like to conserve discussion time by collecting prayer intentions on slips of paper at the beginning and having each person take one home to pray over for the week. Depending on the personality of your group, you may do more eating, fellowshipping, and general discussion than talking over every question for each chapter. That's fine.

Can participants come to class if they haven't done the reading each week? I hope every group facilitator will challenge and encourage participants to *do* the session heart-work each week. Maybe group members will want to track their progress in a journal; maybe they'll prefer to write in their books. But each chapter's heart-work is short enough that it should always be finished.

Because we are all way too busy, you will inevitably run across those who come to community meetings without their *An Invitation* and *God Prompt* sections completed. Participants who have not completed the heart-work should still be encouraged to come because they will get a lot out of the group discussion. Still, there is no substitute for an engaged participant. I hope you will not only pray for each of your participants, but also encourage them to complete each chapter, since each one gets the women immediately in touch with God in the scriptures.

How to facilitate a good discussion. Creating a welcoming environment is important. Make sure there are enough seats for everyone in the group, and consider arranging seats facing one another in a circle or other inclusive way.

When it's time to pray together, try to guide prayer intentions and sharing so that everyone who wants to is able to participate, but do so without pushing participants to respond or share. Nurture this fellowship between the study participants, since it is a great help to learning and feeling as though one is an integral part of the universal Church.

In almost every group there will be a participant who dominates the discussion. You may need to limit this person's comments as charitably as possible, for the benefit of the whole group and time constraints.

Be enthusiastic, but always start and finish on time, helping the last person speaking to reach a point of conclusion if necessary. Follow up with participants if you discern a particular need.

Finally, this book is about the Holy Spirit's action in our lives. Depend on him. You are the facilitator. Your main job is to facilitate sharing and discussion in a way that sets boundaries but is also sensitive to the leading of the Holy

Spirit in his people. He has called you to this task, and he is personally involved in both you and your study group. Blessings, friend!

Notes

Chapter One: What Do You Wish?

1. Pope Francis, "General Audience," St. Peter's Square, August 27, 2014, http://w2.vatican.va/content/francesco/en/audiences/2014/documents/papa-francesco_20140827_udienza-generale.html.

2. "Homily of Pope John Paul II on the Inauguration of his Pontificate," October 22, 1978, http://www.vatican.va/holy_father/john_paul_ii/homilies/1978/documents/hf_jp-ii_hom_19781022_inizio-pontificato_en.html.

Chapter Two: Who Touched Me?

1. *Chronicles of Narnia: The Lion, the Witch and the Wardrobe*, DVD, directed by Andrew Adamson (Walt Disney Pictures, 2005).

2. Attributed to St. Francis de Sales in John Van Auken, *From Karma to Grace* (Virginia Beach: ARE Press, 2010), 110.

3. Simone Weil, *Gravity and Grace* (Lincoln, NE: Bison Books, 1997) 213.

Chapter Three: Has No One Condemned You?

1. Fr. Reginald Garrigou-Lagrange, O.P., *The Three Ages of the Interior Life, Volume 1* (Rockford, IL: Tan Books 1989), 316.

2. Attributed to Edmund Burke in David Eakin, *The Jethro Priciple* (Nashville, TN: CrossBooks 2014), 27.

3. Scott Peck, MD, *The Road Less Traveled* (New York: Touchstone, 2003), 15.

4. Attributed to St. Augustine in Fr. George Haydock, *Duay Rheims Old Testament of the Holy Catholic Bible with Comprehensive Catholic Commentary* (Moravia, CA: Catholic Treasures 1992), Eccl 11:3.

5. St. John of the Cross, *Dichos* (Washington, DC: ICS Publications 1991), 60.

Chapter Four: Why Do You See the Speck in Your Neighbor's Eye, but Do Not Notice the Log in Your Own Eye?

1. St. Catherine of Siena, *Dialogue* (Mahwah, NJ: Paulist Press 1980), 33, 38.

Chapter Five: Why Do You Call Me "Lord, Lord" but Not Do What I Command?

1. C. S. Lewis, *The Problem of Pain* (San Francisco, CA: HarperOne, 2003), 93.

Chapter Seven: Have You Never Read the Scriptures?

1. Pope Francis, "Recital of the Holy Rosary for the Conclusion of the Marian Month of May," St. Peter's Square, May 31, 2013, http://w2.vatican.va/content/francesco/en/speeches/2013/may/documents/papa-francesco_20130531_conclusione-mese-mariano.html.

2. St. Jerome, *Commentariorum in Isaiam libri* xviii prol: PL 24,17B.

3. Fr. Lawrence G. Lovasik, S.V.D., *The Hidden Power of Kindness* (Manchester, NH: Sophia Institute Press, 1999), 173.

4. Evagrius Ponticus, *De oratione* 35: PG 79, 1173.

5. St. Augustine, *Ep.* 130m 8m 17: PL 33, 500.

6. Pope Francis, "Recital of the Holy Rosary for the Conclusion of the Marian Month of May," St. Peter's Square, May 31, 2013, http://w2.vatican.va/content/francesco/en/speeches/2013/may/documents/papa-francesco_20130531_conclusione-mese-mariano.html.

For Group Reading and Study

1. Remember, members of your group may be reading from different versions of the Catholic scriptures. When reading and studying the Bible, it is helpful to compare different versions because differences in word selection and translation contribute to our understanding of what the verses mean.

Sonja P. Corbitt is a dynamic Catholic author, speaker, and broadcaster who has produced several high-impact, uplifting multimedia Bible studies, including *Soul of the World*, *Fearless*, and *Ignite*.

A Carolina native who was raised as a Southern Baptist, Corbitt attended Mitchell College and the Southern Baptist Seminary Extension and then converted to Catholicism. She served as director of religious education at St. John Vianney Catholic Church in Gallatin, Tennessee, and as executive director of Risen Radio in Lebanon, Tennessee.

Corbitt broadcasts a daily radio show on Real Life Radio called *Pursuing the Summit*. She is in formation as a Third Order Carmelite and is a columnist at *Catholic Online*. She has appeared numerous times on radio and television and wrote for the *Gallatin News Examiner* and *Oremus*, the Westminster Cathedral magazine. She lives in Tennessee with her husband, Bob, and two sons. Her website is www.pursuingthesummit.com.

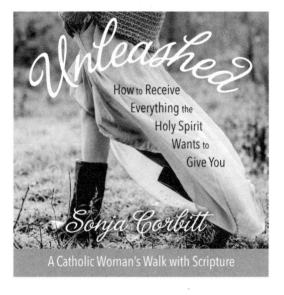